DR. A. T. STILL
FOUNDER OF
OSTEOPATHY

By

M. A. LANE

*Professor of Pathology in the American School
of Osteopathy at Kirksville*

Published by
THE OSTEOPATHIC PUBLISHING CO.
CHICAGO

DR. ANDREW TAYLOR STILL
FOUNDER OF OSTEOPATHY

CONTENTS

CONTENTS

CONTENTS

CONTENTS

FOREWORD

Believing that the time is auspicious for publishing an appreciation of Dr. Still's work and a study of the place he occupies, and will continue to occupy for all time, in the history of medicine, the publishers looked around some time ago to select an author in all ways capable of writing such a study and an appreciation, and we were fortunate enough to secure the willing service of a man whose own life work has eminently fitted him for the task—a man who came into osteopathy several years ago with an already established international reputation for his own original researches in pure biological science, and who is today devoting his life to original research in osteopathy and the scientific teaching of the osteopaths of the future. We refer to M. A. Lane, professor of pathology in the American School of Osteopathy at Kirksville, and director of the post-graduate laboratory there for clinical diagnosis. Professor Lane's name and discoveries are familar to the students of medicine in all the great university schools of medicine in this country and Europe. They were discussed with high praise by Professor Ernest LaGuesse of the University of Lille, France, at the International Medical Congress at Buda-Pesth in 1908; they are recorded in the new text-book of Professor Biedl, professor of internal secretions at the University of Vienna; in the new text-book of applied anatomy of the late Baron Treves, the foremost of British surgeons, and late surgeon to the King; in the new text-book of Starling, the foremost of English physiologists; in the new text-book of Professor Stewart, the foremost of British-American physiologists; in the new text-book of pathology of Professor Mallory of Harvard University Medical School, the foremost American pathologist; in the new text-book of histology of Professor Ferguson; in the review of the world's research work by Dr. Albert Oppel, of the University of Halle, a foremost authority in Germany and in Europe and America. Professor Lane has written these chapters on Doctor Andrew Taylor Still and his place in medicine with the pen of a man whose touches are sure and true, whose insight comes from practical and precise knowledge, and whose acquaintance with the historical development of medical science is inferior to that of no American writer on these subjects. In these analyses we see the "Old Doctor" rising to the full measure of his scientific stature; we see for the first time the complete articulation of osteopathy with the scientific progress of the age, and we see, again for the first time, portrayed the fundemental rock upon which Andrew Taylor Still laid down his science and art when he gave osteopathy to the world. Although the contents of this book were written for publication as ten independent articles, each discussing a phase of Dr. Still's work, they articulate naturally without revision when grouped as chapters in a book, revealing only slight evidence here and there of repeating a statement or allusion, which of course, would not have been the case had the author written his matter in the first place for publication as a book.

—THE PUBLISHERS

A. T. STILL AS A MEDICAL THINKER

In order to comprehend osteopathy we must comprehend the work of Andrew Taylor Still, and to that end we must know in a clear way something of the immediate predecessors of the man, together with something of the medical world upon which the eyes of A. T. Still opened and into which they looked with the sharpest criticism of the ages.

Improvement in human institutions comes about by two methods, which are in reality two aspects of one fundamental fact. These two are reform and revolution. Reform is slow, revolution rapid; but the results accomplished by both are essentially and practically the same. Fundamental and original discoveries in science are always revolutionary in their effects, as are also fundamental perceptions in art.

Now medicine is an art, and when we discuss "reform" in medicine we are compelled to look at our subject from two separate and distinct points of view—namely, the changes that have come about because of discoveries in pure science—which have only an incidental bearing on the practice of the art of medicine—and changes that are instituted by the actual practitioner of medicine himself apart from the discoveries of pure science.

In examining the history of medicine, only one practitioner can be found who combined the two things in himself; who used pure science as his primary method and directly based his practice upon it. This man was Andrew Taylor Still, whose reform of medicine was revolutionary—therefore rapid—and radical to the very roots of the entire structure itself.

MEDICINE'S SLOW PAINFUL REFORM

Previously to Still, medical practitioners had honestly tried to reform their art, and suffered the fate of the reformer in consequence. The first great reformer in what we call modern medicine was Flaubert, the French physician of the latter end of the 18th and the beginning of the 19th Century. Medicine in his day was a procedure of purge, vomit, blistering, bleeding, and a mixture of materia medica drawn from nauseating substances of all kinds, and from plants, the virtues of which were based upon absolute superstition— the entire art in that day being but slightly more scientific or civilized than the practice of the savage tribe with its medicine man.

Not one of the physiological beliefs of the physicians of Flaubert's time survives in the present day.

Flaubert failed to make the slightest impression on the medical craft of his age. He made no appeal to science. There was no science, save anatomy, in that time with a direct bearing on medical practice. Such reform as he attempted was nothing but a protest against every one of the agents and every method of treatment then in use as therapeutic. In a word, Flaubert sought to dismantle medicine as he had found it. Small wonder he failed in a day when the art of medicine had as little true understanding of the real body as could possibly be, if we neglect the imperfect work of the anatomists of the time, of Harvey on the circulation and of Hunter on the coagulation of the blood. Flaubert had in him the same medical nihilism as Still had when he looked around and saw that "the patients we were treating for disease were dead". But in the hands of the French physician medical nihilism was futile, whereas in the hands of Still it led to the only general therapy the world has ever known.

HAHNEMANN, THE SECOND REFORMER

The second attempt in the modern reform of medicine by practitioners was made by Hahnemann, the founder of the homeopathic school, who, quite unlike Flaubert, was anything but a medical nihilist. Hahnemann's great principle was based on the two main beliefs, first, that drugs of any kind (or any other kind of substance) which, when introduced into the body, would produce symptoms similar to those of the disease to be cured, would effect that cure; and secondly, that the smaller the dose of the drug used the more vigorous would be the physiological (curative) effect of it. The first belief became a kind of motto with the homeopaths—"Like is cured by like."

This system of therapy in its practical application was in reality the abandonment of internal medicine altogether, for in the high dilutions given

3

all physiological effect vanished. Hahnemann succeeded, without wishing to do so, in abolishing drugs, although he believed that he was using drugs in stronger form than ever. A glance at the materia medica of the homeopaths is sufficient to produce nausea in a person with a "delicate stomach," or in other words with psychic tendency to sea sickness.

HELPED BY WEAKENING THE DOSE

Hahnemann not only swallowed the entire ancient apothecary's shop, but vastly multiplied the number of drugs in use by the old "regular" school. It is difficult to believe that any homeopath today can take himself seriously in the matter of "high potency" dilutions, although human credulity can stretch ad infinitum. Certainly in these days of scientific pharmacology and physiology, of pathology and immunology, one would imagine that "old time homeopathy" should be a thoroughly dead cock in the pit. Hahnemann's reform, however, was the best "practical" reform up to its own time, for it saved many a life by indirection. The medicines could literally do no harm, a fact to which Osler attributed homeopathic "cures".

ECLECTICISM THE THIRD REFORM

The third great reform practitioner was Bennett, the Scotchman, who reacted in the other direction. Bennett founded what he called the Eclectic School, that is, the "choosing" school. Any remedy whether homeopathic or "allopathic" (a name ever repudiated by the ancient school of physicians) that was proved good would be used by the eclectics. But Bennett was compelled to put a new shine on the old drugs, so he decided to extract the drug in a fresh rather than in a dry state, making the drug more active, as he believed —an absurdity on its face to those who know. But Bennett did better than all this. He was probably the first reformer who by his opposition compelled the old doctors to abandon the bleeding methods in general use in his time.

Thus far we see that every useful reform in modern medicine was in the direction of destroying whatever therapy the art of medicine had inherited from the ages, rather than in creating or discovering a new therapy underpinned by scientific fact.

A. T. STILL, M. D., BROUGHT A SCIENTIFIC THERAPY

And then, on the heels of Bennett came Still, the fourth and last reformer of eminence of modern medical art, with a therapy which automatically abolished all previous practiced therapy by positive, not negative, methods of treatment. Osteopathy had been discovered.

An amazing fact in the history of medicine is this, that from the time of the discovery of the valves in the veins by Fabricio ab Aquapendente (which led to the discovery of the circulation of the blood by Harvey) down to 1890 when Behring, working in Koch's Laboratory, discovered the antitoxins, not one experimental result of real science had ever been successfully applied to the cure of any disease in man or in animal! What an in-

stupendous fact! From Harvey to Behring scientific investigation with its infinite printed matter in our knowledge of the conduct of living matter, had resulted in positively nothing in the way of therapy! Can you wonder that osteopathy, when it came, was a success? The panorama of Europe's great scientific progress in all the biological sciences accomplished nothing except to strike down, one after another, every medical agent, every therapeutic fallacy that had come down from a past black with superstition and death, and every one that had sprung up since the Italian Renaissance. Medicine, it was seen, was only a hideous nightmare, rescued during the ages from the dismal superstitution of the jungle and the primitive imagination of the brute man, who filled the earth and the air with the deities and the devils of his childlike and fearsome brain.

With these truths clearly before us we can understand the work done by Still, and can comprehend why osteopathy is!

We can understand how this therapy, vital from its first conception, has remained vital and will continue to live and do its work even in spite of the fact that its practitioners and its researchers have not been able to interpret it with that detail and precision that is scientifically desirable.

Still's entire therapy rests on two grand generalizations which, like all revolutionary discoveries in science, were at first totally incomprehensible to the thought of the age upon which they dawned. To measure their revolutionary character we must remember in what the medical be-

dictment of the art of medicine there lies in that
lief of that day consisted. The cure of disease in
that time was limited in the main to internal medicine. By that is meant the putting into the body
— into the blood and the tissues — substances
called "medicines" because they were believed to
heal the body. In 1870 disease was just beginning
to be studied. Virchow had just dawned with the
discovery of the modern science of pathology.
Until Virchow's work nobody had the slightest
understanding of the nature of disease itself.
Pathology was only a name. The best scientists
of Europe knew as little—far less indeed—of disease than the average intelligent layman of today
who reads the popular magazines. Neither scientists nor physicians had the slightest suspicion
that many diseases were caused by the growth in
the tissues or the blood, or in both, of the parasitic
organisms so well understood today. Tumors were
mere "lumps" growing in the body, some of which
resembled normal tissues. Skin eruptions of every
kind were believed to be "impurities" of the blood,
and the people swallowed oceans of drugs believed
to be "blood purifiers". Patients with fevers were
generously bled even as late as 1870. At that time
purging and vomiting were the usual practice.
The quantities of mercury salts sold by prescription and without prescription would stagger the
intelligence of today. Quinine was handled com-
mercially by the ton as a staple to the people. It
was swallowed by the ton, with and without prescription, by all persons, from babes to centenar-
ian, in all febrile conditions. The wholesale drug

trade was one of the most important divisions of civilized human activity. Drug stores were drug stores then.

A little scientific pathology would have remedied these evils, but of scientific pathology there was none! Virchow was only a dim blaze on the horizon of things. Let us repeat: The theory back of the use of the drug was that some kind, or any kind of substance, taken into the body would or could work a cure. In the very midst of this dismal credulity came A. T. Still, M. D., with this message: The body itself contains within itself all the chemicals, all the medicines, necessary for the cure of disease.

This assertion was, as you can see, subversive of every belief then current in medicine, but only a moment's thought is necessary to understand how true it was, and how true it is today, and how it had to be from the dawn of life in this old world. There is hardly a disease that is invariably fatal. No disease invariably kills all the individuals whom it attacks. Indeed the vast majority of human beings and animals are normally in the act of continuously "curing themselves" of disease by which they are being continuously "attacked". Were this not true all races of animals including man, would swiftly be destroyed by the various biological reactions which ignorance had named disease. The sciences of histology, pathology, immunology and pathological chemistry, in the past 30 years, have told us what disease is, and in this modern definition of disease we find that it is only a chemical reaction of one or another kind among the molecule-complexes, or atom-complexes, of which living matter consists.

Thus at one swift stroke of his clear intellectual vision—A. T. Still saw the biological basis upon which modern pathology, in its histological, immunological and chemical aspects, has been reared since the appearance of Virchow and Pasteur. Credit for this original and far-reaching perception—the perception of a mind of prime origination and imperial power—will be given to Still in due time by the future historians of our sciences. The earlier pupils of Still could see the force of the truth he taught them, because they themselves had been born and bred in the midst of the medical ideas of Still's own age. And these early pupils will recall how bitterly this fundamental truth was fought, how viciously it was ridiculed by the medical men of that time and later. Today this fact is taught in every university in the world as one of the fundamental bases of a superior and scientific medical education.

TRUTH USUALLY OBVIOUS AFTER BEING PROCLAIMED

One of the great arms of Still's new system of therapy was therefore the principle of the general immunity of the blood and the tissue to disease, and so self-evident is the truth of this principle that the wonder is it was not seen ages before the time of Still and his pupils.

Why do the sick recover?

Answer, because the body is self-healing.

Why is the body self-healing?

Answer, because only those organisms that had

in them the necessary chemical and structural elements for resistance to so-called disease survived in the struggle for existence during the long and tragic life-history of the past. Because only those organisms that had these necessary elements of resistance and recovery from disease, could live long enough to reproduce their kind, thus passing down to the new generation the self-healing and self-adjusting mechanisms that safeguard the maintenance of the races we see inhabiting the earth today.

But if this is true, why is there any disease today in men and animals? Why are not the surviving races entirely free from disease?

Answer, because for the survival of a race it was essential only that the self-healing mechanisms would enable a few of the race to live long enough to reproduce its kind. Absolute immunity to all diseases in all organisms was not a condition of survival.

But it is clear that if immunity in some or in a few were not general against all death-dealing diseases, there could have been no recovery of any organism whatsoever, and hence there had been no survival, whatsoever, and life had ceased long ago.

ALL LATE RESEARCH SUPPORTS STILL'S THEORIES

Still clearly perceived the necessity of general immunity against all diseases, including the tumors, but he did not derive his principle from the agreement above outlined, because in his day the facts of development as discovered by Darwin and Wallace were mainly unknown to the world at large, and not understood at all or accepted by the great body of scientific men who, on the contrary, ridiculed the law of natural selection as an altogether too simple thing to account for the facts of life. If today that law is universally taught as a fact, it is only because it was a discovery of prime character. And if Still's great principle has been proved to be absolutely true by the world's researches of the past 25 years, it is only because it was true when he announced it, and hence destined to be proved experimentally some day, soon or late. In short, his principle had to be tested by the fire of experimental science and experimental criticism, and how well it has come through untouched in any phase of its integrity by these tests, it has been my privilege and my happiness to study and to know.

RESULTS PROVE OSTEOPATHY SUCCESSFUL AS A THERAPY

But Sill's principle has been passing through another and a different kind of criticism and test during the years that have followed its announcement. I mean it has been tested by the practical experience of the pupils of Still's school in the actual treatment of disease. Osteopaths love to point to their results, past and present, as the living proof of the truth of Still's theory in its twofold form. For Still, studying anatomy, had the rare power of perception to see that the backbone is the keystone of the body, and that this imperial palace of the imperial tissue of the body— the nerve—was the source of constant disturbance of the circulation of the blood. The nerves as well as all the other tissues of the body, live in an ocean of blood (or lymph, that comes from the blood) and the back-bone through its innumerable slips and mal-adjustments does and must produce innumerable disturbances of circulation. Hence the second arm of Still's theory—the osteopathic lesion. Accepting this theory from the mind of Still, osteopaths worked whole heartedly with it as their main if not the only tool of healing, with what results the whole world knows.

I sometimes think that the spirit of Andrew Taylor Still will return upon many osteopaths who have lost faith in that old back-bone lesion as the main causative factor in disease, and will annihilate their skepticism. These modern skeptics, these doubters of the truth of Still's back-bone lesion theory of disease, live and grow prosperous on that theory while they doubt the truth of it in their hearts.

OSTEOPATHY FOUNDED UPON BACKBONE LESION ADJUSTMENT

Let such doubters and skeptics remember that the earlier osteopaths succeeded in winning the faith of the public in osteopathy only because they preached that back-bone lesion day and night. Let them remember that if it were not for that imperial generalization of A. T. Sill, there would be no osteopathy today. Let them remember that every patient they treat, they must treat by the backbone method, or lose that patient. Let them remember that every new patient that comes to osteopathy for treatment expects that treatment in the main. (I am not now speaking of sprained

ankles, broken noses, or obvious traumatisms in
parts other than the spine. I am speaking of disease in general.) What treatment have you, gentlemen, for diseases in general other than spinal
treatment based on Still's lesion? And if you point
to the glorious record of osteopathy, do you not
point to the osteopathic spinal bony-tissue lesion
as the cause of that record? And if you win your
share of success by treating the spine are you not
at least an unintelligent operator (if not a self-
stultifier) when you repudiate the great secondary
principle of which osteopathy consists? Are you
waiting until the scientists of the world have put
their experimental approval also on this back-bone
etiology? Are you waiting until, through the dic-
tum of the world's men of science, the whole
medical profession have adopted the back-bone
lesion as the main causative factor in disease, and
have taken over your therapy to themselves—are
you waiting for this until you become real osteopaths, osteopaths in mind as well as in fingers?
If you are, you can rest assured that you will not
have long to wait. We are living in an age of
revolution, and Still's medical revolution is at the
world's door today.

But again, science itself is not without the evidence that the spinal lesion is the main factor in
the causation of disease. And this evidence is
quite as axiomatic in the matter of Still's spinal
lesion as it is in the matter of Still's law of general immunity. Is it necessary to bring forward
scientific evidence that spinal etiology is true? Is
it necessary to do this to convince the osteopath?

Any osteopath? If so, what has such an osteopath been doing? What becomes of the entire osteopathic therapy? I will tell you what becomes of it. It vanishes like the dream of a fool into that limbo of hideous dreams on the other side of the moon! The world would be well rid of it, and the thousands of men, women, and children who have been cured by it have been victims of a moonshine psychology.

ZOOLOGY WILL SUPPORT THE LESION THEORY

Our grand old man in his life-time was disturbed by no such fears, and science is as able to demonstrate the truth of the second great principle he discovered as it has been to demonstrate the truth of the first.

The osteopathic lesion as a general factor in the etiology of disease is grounded on the same scientific basis as is Still's theory of general immunity to disease, and is destined surely to be accepted, in the end, by specialists in zoology and hence in the facts of natural selection—the great and fundamental law of life and of matter itself; next by the specialists in pathology, a science that is utterly incomprehensible unless studied and interpreted in the light of that great law of natural selection; and lastly by the medical profession itself, the individual members of which are trained by these specialists in the fundamental sciences pertaining to the structures and the work of the animal body. But before Still's spinal lesion can be accepted by the medical profession as the main causative factor in disease—a cause that interferes with the so-called "normal" conduct of the body—that spinal lesion in all its significance must be studied by the zoologists, the physiologists, the physiological chemists, the pharmacologists, and the pathologists of all kinds, and its importance in the life history of races mastered and understood.

THERE IS NO OTHER GENERAL THERAPY TODAY!

There is no general therapy today, there never has been a general therapy, excepting osteopathy, based on these two great generalizations of Andrew Taylor Still—the law of the general immunity of organisms to so-called disease, and the law of the spinal lesion as the main ultimate etiological factor in that great tribe of animals called the vertebrates.

But you may say, how about the vast hordes of animals that are not vertebrates, that have no backbones? Are they to be without a therapy? Did not Still think of them, too, in his grand scheme of healing?

The answer is simple. He did not. Still had in his hands only a man. But you will observe that the invertebrates, plants as well as animals, are in perfect harmony with the law of general immunity which Still announced for the human species. A. T. Still was not a "materialistic" thinker. He believed, as was natural in his day, in a kind of "divine" supervision of nature, or perhaps in the divinity of nature itself—a belief or conviction to which many men of advanced science are coming back today, and so forward has become the scientific mind that a Thomson, a Ramsey, a Becquerel and a Still could meet on common ground and understand one another's philosophical conceptions of nature and the "soul" of nature. The very fact that Still in his science of disease and its remedy did not take into account the invertebrate world, and calculated chiefly if not wholly the human element, lends additional value to his discoveries. Science has demonstrated his law of immunity in all living things, as well as in man. If what he held of man be true, it must be true for all other forms of life. Were it not true for all other forms, it could not be true for man. The very test of its truth in the case of man was its universal application to all living things. And in the past 25 years it has been proved universally true by the laboratories of Europe. His theory concerning the spinal lesion as the main primary causative factor in disease must stand a similar test. It must be true not only in the case of man, but also in that of all other vertebrates. And he who adequately studies comparative pathology in the light of the law of natural selection will not for one minute combat the theory of the spinal lesion in that etiological sense because he perceives the necessity of its truth. To these osteopaths who have doubts as to the virtue of that theory as a primary conception in their art, I would recommend a careful study of the literature of evolution and comparative embryology and can guarantee them that their convictions will then square with their practice.

This original theory of A. T. Still has been steadfastly taught to the young osteopaths that have been trained in the American School of Osteopathy at Kirksville. It has been instilled in their minds at that school from the beginning. It has been consistently taught them during the years I have been myself a teacher in that school, and when it ceases to be taught there the American School of Osteopathy will be no longer a representative of the essential and fundamental thought of its founder. No school that does not make that theory the main spring and purpose of its existence can be called osteopathic without false pretense and the moral and scientific obliquity that false pretense of any kind implies. And when osteopathy lets go of that primary teaching it ceases to be.

II

A. T. STILL SCIENTIST AND REFORMER

The key to the work of Andrew Taylor Still in his capacity as a scientific reformer was his unusually and powerfully original mind. Like all men of surpassing genius his one great dominant characteristic was his strong and active originality. He was by nature entirely unfitted to follow in beaten paths those who had gone before him. To strike out in new directions, to carve for himself with his own hammer and chisel the block of knowledge, theory and practice, was for him a necessity; and few of the many theories he held were borrowed from or suggested by his predecessors in the art of medicine. He appeared on the stage of medicine when that art was just on the verge of the searching and universal scientific reforms that were destined soon to change the entire point of view with which men, up to that time, had been accustomed to regard their own bodies in health and disease. But in his earlier days established medical practice was almost as barbaric and ancient as it had ever been since the age of the great Greek school of physicians in the time of Pericles, five hundred years before Christ.

When Dr. Still was a young man, speculating on the cause of cholera, many of the great scientific discoveries and epoch-making inventions in the

18

art of medicine were just in the making, or were being one by one announced to an astonished and unbelieving world. That was the day when Europe was yet ringing with the freshly announced discoveries of Theodor Schwann, who was the first to see and announce the fact that the bodies of all animals were built up of cells—the so-called "Cell Theory" of Schwann, a theory which, like Ehrlich's theory of immunity, soon passed into the realm of undisputed fact. That was the day when the new pathology—the cellular pathology—was germinating in the mind of the great Virchow, who has been rightly called "the father of pathology"; when the powerful Louis Pasteur was doing his best thinking in the remarkable controversies concerning life and its origin that were then raging in Europe, with Liebig on the one side and Pasteur on the other; when Helmholtz was forging in his mathematical workshop the law of the conservation of energy, and reducing to demonstrable fact the conception that living bodies were chemical and physical machines in which energy was transformed but never lost; when Johannes Mueller, the father of modern physiology, at the very apex of his career, was about to pass away; when the term "irritability of living matter" was refreshingly and startlingly new; when the chemists of Germany and France were discovering the marvelous facts of organic compounds, and searching by synthesis and analysis into the secrets of living nature; when the theory of "vital force" was rapidly disappearing out of the minds of scientific thinkers; when Darwin was forging the links of his great chain of natural selection; when von Baer was first perceiving the amazing facts and their laws of the new-born science of embryology; when Haeckel was observing (for the first time) the fact that the white cells of the blood had the power of ingesting small particles of dead matter—the first perception of the "phagocytosis" of Metchnikoff; when Claude Bernard, the French physiologist, was announcing his theory that all substances that could enter the body were to be regarded as either foods or poisons; when pepsin was being discovered by Schwann, and the structure of the kidney by Henle; when, in one word, the whole scientific world was in a state of ferment, in which wholly new views and facts about living matter were being upturned and established every day, and the old foundations on which medicine had been resting for ages were being rapidly and surely dissolved away. It was in such an age that A. T. Still appeared.

ANTICIPATED THE BEST SCIENTIFIC THINKING OF EUROPE

When Dr. Still was beginning to see clearly through his newly formed ideas of therapy and the causes of diseases in general, the science of modern pathology was in its infancy, and the science of bacteriology, as we know it today, was as yet virtually undreamed of; the science of physiology was only just beginning to show its first and broadest outlines; and the sciences of histology and embryology were only beginning to be understood in their more startling details; and we can say with absolute truth that Dr. Still was the only man in America who could in any way whatever be regarded as being abreast with the spirit of Europe; rather let us say he was, in many of his primary conceptions, forty years ahead of Europe and his age, a fact which we will try to show here, and a fact which will be amply recognized in the history of medicine as it will be written in the time to come.

To appreciate Dr. Still's true inherent greatness, it is necessary to roll back the years, to reverse history, and to realize to ourselves the medical doctor of that early day, especially in the United States. Dr. Still's earlier life—say until he was 50 years old—was lived in a time when medicine in America had cut itself entirely adrift from the medical education of Europe. In the earlier years of the nineteenth century the American physician was always educated in Europe, and in those primitive times, reaching back into the later years of the eighteenth century, some of the most famous anatomists of Europe paid now and then visits to these shores. In Philadelphia there still stands, or stood until recently, an anatomical theatre, where anatomists exhibited and lectured to the lay public on handsome dissections of the human body, as had been the custom in Europe. Those were the times when no medical schools existed in America, and all American physicians were educated abroad. With the rise of the first medical colleges in America, however, this custom ceased, and toward the middle of the last century, America was educating her own doctors, who, in the beginning, were almost as well informed as their European colleagues. But this equality of education soon passed away, and from then onwards medical education in America was distinctly inferior to that of Europe. The American medical colleges passed into the hands of American doctors who had themselves never studied in Europe, and the result was that hundreds of medical schools of inferior type sprang up in this country, and American medicine was now upon an American basis, and a basis much lower, of course, than that of the great universities of Europe, where the newer medical sciences were being born and developed. Hence there was in America scarcely a handful of physicians of a high scientific type. There were no discoveries made in America, and such medicine as was here was of the distinctly old style, crude and backward, and loaded with many of the superstitious beliefs and practices that had marked the medicine of Europe before the days of Schwann and Pasteur, of von Baer and Raymond, of Virchow and Helmholtz, of Bowman and Henle, of Mueller and Bernard and of the other pure scientists whose work did so much to place medicine on a pedestal higher than that of mere experience or empiricism. American doctors were notably behind the procession of Europe, and only here and there could be found a doctor with any appreciation at all of the medical reforms that were going forward so rapidly in the universities on the other side of the sea. To this rule, surgery was something of an exception. American surgery was always good, but surgery is a thing distinctly apart from medicine, and in so far as the doctor was a surgeon he was not a physician at all.

Such was the state of medicine in America when Dr. Still appeared, with entirely new conceptions and theories concerning diseases, their causes and cures. In the west of the United States, far remote from the slightest influence of Europe, in the midst of the black ignorance and incompetence of American uneducated doctors, grew up this singular reformer, who, had he risen in Europe, would have exerted the most powerful world-wide influence from the very first.

HIS TWO GREAT DISCOVERIES, LESIONS AND IMMUNITY

Like all great original thinkers, Dr. Still had theories for almost every disease and function of the body, and many of these theories were crude and incompetent, just because the then state of the sciences he dealt with was still crude and incompetent. In fact, when Dr. Still worked out many of his theories of disease, the real causes of these diseases were wholly unknown and seemingly incomprehensible. But of the various theories which, like sparks from a grinding wheel, flew off from his original and ever-active mind, at least two were of prime order and absolutely true and good. These were first, his theory of the mechanical (anatomical) lesion, and secondly, his theory of the chemical immunity of the body, both of which he put forth as the cause of disease, and both of which have absolutely stood the test of time and subsequent scientific criticism and experiment. The scientific historian of the future, who will write at a time when all prejudices of professional jealousy and hate will have been lost in the great historical perspective, will probably regard Dr. Still's greatest contribution to science as being his theory of immunity rather than his wonderful perception of the mechanical origin of so-called disease. For it is a fact that while the great conception of the osteopathic lesion was directly responsible for the grand dramatic debut of osteopathy and its seemingly miraculous cures, more recent knowledge and understanding of osteopathic treatment and its results have called attention in a striking and startling way to Dr. Still's other grand and primary conception of the body's natural immunity; a conception primary in every sense of that word; for it is upon this great fact of nature that the osteopathic lesion, with all it means to the osteopath and the diseases he works in, hangs. Dr. Still in his own mind and his own writings placed this great natural immunity of the body first in order, and then followed it up with the correction of the lesion, by which procedure the defensive and hence curative mechanism of the body was given free play.

WAS FIRST TO ANNOUNCE THE THEORY OF IMMUNITY

In justice to the original mind of this American genius, it should be said that Dr. Still was the first man to perceive the truth that nature has developed in the animal body its own defences against diseases. And with this thought in mind we can for the first time see the power and real meaning in his well worn axiom, "Find it, fix it, and leave it alone!"

The three last words contain the heart of the axiom—leave it alone; because by leaving it alone, Dr. Still most certainly did not mean that the practitioner should never touch his patient again! What he did mean was that after the lesion has been corrected nature itself will do all the necessary subsequent work—that is, it is not necessary (nay, it is hurtful) to thrust into the body the drugs that, in his day, were believed by all doctors of all schools to have some effect against the disease at work in the body. "Leave it alone" is nothing but a vigorous protest against drug treatment which in Dr. Still's time was the only treatment for any and all diseases which the surgeons' knife could not remove.

OSTEOPATHY AVAILABLE IN THE INFECTIOUS DISEASES

While it is perfectly true, and rightly so, that the osteopath in the past has seemed to rest his entire dependence upon the anatomical lesion (because it was in the correction of these lesions that osteopathy in the beginning worked its most amazing results), it is none the less true that by persistent effort the osteopath has swept under his control dieases which the earlier osteopaths were disposed to neglect as being, in some way or other, outside the domain of the anatomical lesion. Today in the great center and mother institution of osteopathy at Kirksville, a city made world renowned by Dr. Still and the system of therapy he founded, there are young osteopaths, yet in the student stage of their career, who, with entire confidence in their own power and the science under it, treat all kinds of infectious diseases with a courage, or rather with an entire want of fear, that reminds one of the primitive Christians.

EUROPEAN RESEARCH HAS CONFIRMED STILL'S TEACHINGS

All these facts are individual little monuments to the genius of A. T. Still, because they show how well he anticipated the discoveries of the world's most enlightened and capable scientists of later years; and if Europe, with the genius of its laboratories, has given to the world a better understanding of the causes, the prevention, and the rational theory of the cure of diseases, what it has done is only the scientific demonstration of the theory of disease (the natural defences of the body) which was first perceived and announced as his own theory of disease forty years ago by Andrew Taylor Still. Therefore, we say it is only just to the genius of the man to give to him the credit for having been the first to conceive this theory of immunity to disease, which, during the past twenty-five years, has grown with such rapidity and strength as to fill the whole world with its noise and to change radically all views of diseases and the possibility of their cure.

An extraordinarily high degree of credit should be given him for this remarkable and original perception for the very reason that it came to him at a time when the facts of immunity were not at all understood, nor in any way seen or believed to be concerned with disease in general. At that time, as well as in all previous times, the bare fact of immunity, natural and acquired, was and had been for ages familiar to men. It was a matter of common knowledge and experience that certain diseases in men were followed by immunity to these certain special diseases. It was a fact of common knowledge and experience, for example, that an attack of smallpox was followed by immunity to smallpox in the future; that men perhaps never had a second attack of the disease; that persons having passed through one attack of the disease were universally regarded as being safe against a second attack. Scarlet fever, mumps, yellow fever, measles, and other diseases, called infectious or contagious, were similar to smallpox in their power of conferring immunity against the disease. But this power of conferring immunity was thought to be limited to those diseases alone in which the immunity conferred was lasting throughout the life of the individual. Other diseases, to a second or third or several attacks of which the body was susceptible, were not classified as diseases that immunized the individual. But it is now known that all infectious diseases do produce an immunity, in all ways similar to that produced by smallpox except for the length of time during which the immunity lasts.

If, let us say, pneumonia produces an immunity which safeguards the individual as efficiently as smallpox does, only that the immunity wears out, say in a year or more, you have a similar power to that in smallpox, only the effects do not last a life time. The same is true of typhoid fever, and in-

deed of all infectious diseases. This will be seen
to be necessarily true when it is remembered that
if an immunity, more or less lasting, were not produced by the disease, the disease would never disappear, the patient never "get well". So that it
would appear that all infections act in the body
in a way similar to smallpox but with certain
variations in the length of time during which the
reaction, or the "safety", lasts. This would bring
all infection under the same natural law; but the
proof of these facts means only one thing, and
that is this, that an individual, not immune to a
disease in the first place, but who becomes immune
after the disease has been acquired and "runs its
course" with recovery, must have in his body previously to the attack some kind of mechanism
which the presence of the disease excites to the
formation of substances which now are in sufficient quantity to prevent, for a longer or shorter
time, a second attack of the disease. This in turn
must mean only that the body is equipped by
nature with its own cure for disease and with the
power of preventing further attacks of the same
disease—for a longer or shorter time after the
first attack.

THE BLOOD CARRIES THE BODY'S HEALING

Dr. Still urged virtually this view of disease,
and held that the curative and protecting thing
was to be found in the blood and hence in the tissues, and in this theory, simple as it appears today
to us who are familiar with the researches of
Europe during the past twenty-five years, is to be

found the very first perception of the great law of immunity to disease of almost every kind, including even the tumors. Dr. Still, in effect, urged the theory that all diseases could be scientifically classified with smallpox, and similar immunizing diseases, and that hence all diseases in their cause and cure could be referred back to the blood. His axiom now follows: Remove the cause which stops or clogs the blood flow, or which blocks the nerve which controls the blood flow, and the blood itself will work the cure. "The rule of the artery is supreme."

HIS IMMUNITY GENERALIZATION REQUIRED YEARS TO BE UNDERSTOOD

Now when Dr. Still began to treat diseases on this principle the entire principle itself was not only amazing to the then current ideas of disease, but was also incomprehensible even to the best thought of his time. To bring virtually all diseases under one main principle was, to the science of that day, a complete absurdity. To say that smallpox, tuberculosis, pneumonia, whooping cough, pimples on the face, leprosy, syphilis, typhoid fever, diarrhoea, a "cold" in the head and cancer were one and all referable to the same basic law (the state of the blood) and perhaps curable by the same method, were the whole problem in all its phases mastered, was not only "revolutionary" but was a wildly impossible and clearly absurd theory of disease in its causes and its cure. But let us ask, in the light of the scientific progress of the past quarter of a century just how absurd and impossible it really was?

Since that time the clear sun of science has risen higher and higher every day to dissipate the darkness that shrouded disease up to the day of Still and his discovery. Rather say, sun after sun of science has risen in succession to that first illuminating discovery of Dr. Still. Metchnikoff rose to show how the white cells of the blood ingest disease germs, ridding the body of these destructive agents, and indeed normally preventing the onset of infections; Buchner, the German bacteriologist, rose, showing how ferments could be separated from the organisms that made them; Uhlenhut rose, to show through his pupil Nuttall, how disease germs, multiplying in the animal body, produced in the blood of the animal a substance that could kill the germs that produced it; Pfeiffer, another German, rose to show how the serum of an animal inocculated with typhoid or cholera germs would dissolve typhoid or cholera germs, but no other; Behring, the pupil of the great Koch, rose to show how the poisons of bacteria could produce in the body of the animal into which they were injected a counter substance which could neutralize and render harmless the toxins themselves, calling them anti-toxins; Bordet, the Frenchman, rose to show how these laws applied to the blood cells of other animals when injected into an experimental animal; Ehrlich rose, to show why all these things had to be true and how the mechanism of the body did its work in the cure and prevention of disease; and finally Abderhalden, the youngest of this array of scientists, rose to show how the tumors were to be classified in their general laws with the

disease germs, so called, the bacteria of the bacteriologists. Limb after limb of the great problem
has been brought under control and more or less
understood, and today not to subscribe in full to
the principle first laid down by Andrew Taylor
Still forty years ago, is to confess one's self as
having no knowledge or understanding at all of
the progress made by biological science within the
past twenty-five years, or (we can say to the uninformed critics of osteopathy) to confess one's
self a person with no knowledge or understanding
of Andrew Taylor Still and his theory.

With these facts in mind we can see A. T. Still
as the original discoverer of one of the great
natural laws of living matter, comparable in all
ways with other great generalizations, the first
perceptions of which were necessarily incomplete
so far as actual demonstration by experiment or
mathematical calculation is concerned. This theory of Still is deserving of being ranked, within
its own special compass, beside the theory of the
chemical and physical basis of life—a theory that
grew in many minds rather than in one. It is,
indeed, a corollary of Darwin's law of natural
selection, for it is clear that if all living organisms
had not been preserved through their ancestral
immunity to disease—through this self-protecting
mechanism that saved them from disaster and
death by disease—they had never survived at all,
the very fact of their survival being of itself in-
disputable evidence of the presence in their bodies
of a defensive and curative force—the old vis
medicatrix naturae (the healing force of nature)

of the ancient doctors that was ever active and automatically self-adjusting under favorable conditions. To re-establish these favorable conditions, when accident had removed them, was the method proposed by Still for the cure of disease; a method absolutely original with himself, and grounded on the most conspicuous fact of human consciousness — the tendency of some forms of living matter to antagonize and destroy certain other forms of living matter, and thus to survive in the struggle for life—"disease" being mainly a struggle for life among living forms, as for example, destructive "germs" or tumor cells, on the one hand, and the normal cells of the body on the other.

GREAT THINKERS LAUNCH MANY IDEAS THAT ARE FOUND WRONG

We have said that Still originated many various physiology which have since been found to be intheories concerning normal and pathological adequate or faulty. But in this respect he resembled all other great geniuses in biology and other sciences. The earlier investigators in all sciences were quite outside the truth in many, and indeed in most, of their scientific speculations, and necessarily so. Many osteopaths, while revering the founder of the new system of healing, have seemed to feel, because Still was right in his two grand principles of disease and its therapy, that therefore he should not have been wrong in anything he said about the body and its work, in health and disease. But such osteopaths are shortsighted and unwise. If Dr. Still had been right in all his theories he would not have been human, not worthy of human admiration. His errors, indeed, and he made many, are really a greater glory to his genius than his two great and true discoveries. Dr. Still's very errors would have been accounted discoveries if made by a common man. He lived and worked out his theories forty-five years ago, and earlier. He had thought out a scientific theory to account for the phenomena of cholera, for example, when other men accounted for them by the belief that this disease was a visitation of Providence on the sins of men. His theory of cholera in the light of subsequent discoveries is seen to be untrue, of course, but to originate any kind of a scientific theory at all of this disease in that day was the mark of an original, scientific and profound thinker. His theory of "blood seed", which few of his interpreters have been able to understand, is an identical theory with that of the contemporaries of Theodor Schwann to account for the growth of cells in the body. Dr. Still himself was a contemporary of Schwann, and it is small wonder that the doctors of that day in America could not understand his meaning when he spoke of "blood seed". The American doctors in that day knew nothing of the cell theory of Schwann, or next to nothing.

Now there was in that day current in the higher scientific circles of Europe a theory of "blood seed", but it was not called by that term. It was known as the "blastema theory". There are probably not many doctors in America today who could tell us what the "blastema theory" was. And why should they, when this theory, like Still's "blood seed" theory, was wiped out by the discovery made later that all cells originate from one cell (the ovum), and that no cell arises except as the continuous splitting—by cell division—of previously existing cells? But the "blastema theory" held that there were in the blood countless millions of invisible particles floating in a special fluid, the "blastema", which had the power of growing large and developing into cells. As a matter of fact, there are in nature certain unicellular animals, such as the organisms that cause smallpox, that do actually grow from invisible units so small that they can pass through the pores of a Berkfeld filter. But the cells of the animal body do not grow in just that way, although the original units of cell development actually exist in the egg cell and its descendants in this inconceivably minute form, and it was upon this conception that the German biologist Weissman founded his wonderful theory of inheritance with its "idants", "ids", "determinants" and "biophors". Now Still, and the other contemporaries of Schwann, held that these minute units (afterwards called "gemmules" by Darwin, "granules" by Altmann and "micellae" and "plastidules" by Haeckel and others), actually floated in the blood and furnished the origin of the cells of the body. In that much, of course, Still and the others were in error, but it is at least an indication of the powerfully original mind of Still that he had hit upon a theory going to the very origin of the cell, similar in all respects to that of the best thinkers of Europe of his day. And we

need have no doubt at all that Still, in common
with his American colleagues, had no intimate acquaintance at all with the finer-spun biological
theories of the Europe of that day.

Again we must remember that Still was a doctor
of the old school and that he did not altogether rid
himself, as his followers have done, of all the old
machinery of the older therapy. We must do him
the justice, however, of being consistent in a
thorough way in his rejection of internal drug
medication. Indeed he held that locomotor ataxia
was caused by the mercury administered to the
syphlitic rather than by the disease; but this is
now known not to be true, although in his day that
speculation of his was quite as justifiable as any
other on the cause of tabes dorsalis.

VAGARIES OF OTHER GREAT SCIENTIFIC REFORMERS

It is interesting to observe, however, that of all
the old drastic methods of therapy which were in
full swing in his own day, only one has retained its
vitality, and that is the principle of so-called
"counter-irritants". Blisters and strong irritating
plasters are potent in certain pains and other
symptoms, although the reason why is perfectly
obscure. And this principle of counter irritants
was perhaps the one prominent therapeutic
method of the old time that Still did not abandon.
He believed, in a limited way, in counter irritants
and used them, sometimes with excellent results,
although the results were not always as sure as
the cures he wrought when he stuck to his own
discovery, osteopathy. His scientific errors and

vagaries, however, were remarkably few when compared with the number of similar errors and vagaries of other great scientific reformers of his own day. For example, if we look into the life work of the great Johannes Mueller, founder of modern physiology, and professor of anatomy and physiology in the University of Berlin (while Still was developing his earliest dissatisfactions with medical unwisdom) we will find that perhaps not one of Mueller's wonderful "discoveries"— accepted in that day as true—has stood the test of subsequent investigation. Mueller wrote whole textbooks of physiology (previously to 1850) which consisted wholly of experiments and theories all his own. And yet all that remains of the work of this great genius of science is the one theory of the "specific energy of nerves". But do we say therefore that Johannes Mueller is unworthy the monuments the world has raised to him and of the honor we do him proudly today? No, indeed. For Mueller's scientific errors and "vagaries" form the fundamental rock and cornerstone of modern physiological science, just as the most striking of Still's errors form the fundament of modern drugless therapy, with this difference that Still's theory of immunity has been absolutely demonstrated by every laboratory in Europe, and his practical application of that theory in osteopathy, the American science of mechano-therapy, has given to a suffering humanity a balm unparalleled and unapproached in the history of the human race.

III

DOCTOR STILL AS A THERAPEUTIST

In the first part of this, our study of Dr. A. T.
Still, we looked at him in his capacity as one of
the great original thinkers and reformers in the
sciences called medical. We showed how he was
the first to state outright, in unequivocal and clear
terms, the great theory of immunity, or rather
how A. T. Still was the first to perceive the fact
that immunity applied not only to the diseases
which, up to his time, were regarded as immunizing diseases, but urged in clear terms the univer-
sality of this great modern biological principle in
diseases of every kind. We showed that to him
belongs the credit of having brought all diseases
under one great law—that of body resistence;
how, theoretically, the blood and the tissues themselves contained the cure for diseases of virtually
every kind. We called attention to his wonderful
perception of the fact that by certain mechanical
manipulations of the body structures, especially
those of the spine, this natural resistence to disease could be released from certain obscure inter-
ferences, or increased in quantity in certain other
circumstances, obscure enough in themselves.
Thus rose in his perception the osteopathic lesion,
which, he claimed, was probably at the source of
most, if not all, disturbances of the body called
pathological. And we further called attention to
his logical abandonment of virtually all the older

methods of medication which, in his day, consisted chiefly of drugs, foreign to the substances of which the body consists, all of which he regarded as poisons or hurts to the natural mechanism of the body itself. We have now to study Dr. Still in the practical application of these principles, or, in other words, to study the master at work with the theoretical tools he invented to realize his theories in fact. And in this study we shall find that Dr. Still was an absolute osteopath, consistent in all ways with his main theoretical findings.

PURE OSTEOPATHY MAKES NO APOLOGY FOR CONSISTENCY

The present writer appreciates the difficulties that would confront any man in a study of this kind, for it is hard to separate Dr. Still's own theories and position from those of many of his followers, who have developed the art that he founded, and have made applications of that art in their own way, with their own modifications. We believe, however, that few osteopaths, who have remained osteopathic, and have not become infected with certain delusions that control the minds of many unscientific medical doctors, will disagree with our statements of fact. A fair review of Dr. Still's work will deal only with his main generalizations, neglecting his adventitious speculations on certain phases of physiology which later investigation has diverted widely from the thought that was current in his own day. To remain a pure osteopath was difficult even for the founder himself, but that does not justify the modern osteopath for departing one jot from the main pure osteopathic principles for which A. T. Still stood and which are entirely and altogether responsible for the magnificent success that is the fruit of osteopathy today. It is probable that had Dr. Still remained in active life long enough to have become acquainted with the results of recent scientific research, he had needed no interpreter such as the present writer, but would have been able to vindicate his own early theory and practice with his own pen, as he was fully able to do. And had he so lived and wrought he would have continued the purest osteopath in the profession he fathered.

MANIPULATION IS ITS METHOD OF APPLICATION

You will ask, what do you mean by a pure osteopath? We mean by that term an osteopath who treats disease by manipulating according to osteopathic technique the tissues of the body, especially the tissues that constitute and support the back bone and the nerves that issue between the vertebrae. This manipulation, however, has no hard and fast system, but can and does vary from a single movement by which "sub-luxations", great or small, or any other unusual stress, tension, or deflection may be removed, to a general treatment, in which the entire vertebral column and its anatomical clothes are thoroughly relaxed and readjusted. As long as the osteopath uses his hands in his therapy, he may be called a pure osteopath. The very moment he adopts any other procedure whatever he is no longer using osteopathy. We do not mean by this, as some of the unthinking and uninformed critics of osteopathy imagine, that an osteopath must necessarily be a stupendous fool, who would attempt to stop a hemorrhage from the ears in fracture of the skull by manipulating the back bone, or who would hold that insects do not transmit disease germs, or who would deny any other known and proved fact. To be an osteopath of any intelligence whatsoever implies that the man in practice is a normal, sane human being.

In a strict definition of the term "pure osteopathy", or, as many of us call it for short, "tenfinger osteopathy", we need not exclude the use of rational methods of hygiene or diet, nor indeed any other scientific regimen that would back up pure osteopathic treatment. But the fact of the matter is that many osteopaths extend their definition too far. We do not believe that Dr. Still would have accepted this modern enlargement of his own term. To say that any method which cures disease or which assists nature in recoveries or reactions against disease is osteopathic is not at all true; but we do not understand that Dr. Still has ever held that osteopathy itself, as a general therapeutic agent, was opposed to all kinds of hygiene, diet, sanitation, or therapy other than osteopathic manipulation. To hold such a view would truly be "more royal than the king." And yet until the last word in osteopathic science has been said, and the last possible experiment in osteopathic research has been made, no man can positively assert that pure osteopathic manipulation will not eventually be found to be all that is necessary in the treatment of disease, and by that we mean all diseases, including even the tumors. Nor can this belief be set aside as the dream of the enthusiast. On the contrary, such a belief will emerge from a study of osteopathic results — at least in man — made with a little actual first-hand knowledge of the body in health and disease as a working foundation for the study itself.

THE OSTEOPATH PRODUCES TROPISMS IN THE BODY

Now Dr. Still found that when he laid his hands, in certain definite ways, on the back bone of a man, the body (and mind) of the individual gave back immediate and profound reactions—what the biologists call tropisms; and this one recent biological term tells the biologist absolutely the entire osteopathic story; explains to the biologist absolutely everything that does or can occur when this method is used on the body.

Tropisms are the reactions of an organism to changes in the environment, and the human organism is highly susceptible (in common with all other living things) to such fundamental relations. Profound chemical changes can be brought about in the central nervous system (and hence in the viscera) by stimulation of the nerve endings in the skin. A prolonged cold bath, for example, will cause albumin to appear in the urine.

But Dr. Still found that manipulation, in certain ways, of the spinal column and its dependent tissues produced certain startling and special reactions, and this was strikingly the case whenever there was in the back bone any visible or palpable irregularity or lesion or deflection. His studies of the spinal mechanism led him to the conviction that virtually all so-called diseases, pains, symptoms, and so on, were indirectly caused by these spinal lesions, when other ana-tomical lesions, or displacements, or tensions, or other structural defects, were absent elsewhere. Disease, in this way, quickly resolved itself, in his mind, into two grand divisions—local and sys-temic. It is difficult, often impossible, to find a spinal lesion (of any kind) in a given case. There-fore must we say it does not exist? By no means. The spinal column has been developed into a mechanism which, by its very structure, is subject to continuous bony displacements and to con-tinuous automatic correction of these displace-ments. But this corrective mechanism is by no means perfect, and it is rational to hold that every spine is subject to a certain percentage of dis-placements that do not correct themselves. These displacements may be so fine as to be difficult to find, but it is safe to say they are there neverthe-less.

It must be admitted that in this view of things there is considerable assumption, but such assumption certainly seems warranted when the matter is given sufficient thought, and the more it is studied the higher the warrant becomes. We must not forget, however, that however high the warrant, it is still assumption, but assumption is always necessary in every theory of science. The generic law of the spinal lesion is peculiar to osteopathy, but it must be remembered, too, that osteopathy includes all anatomical lesions other than spinal. It is hardly necessary to state that fact.

With these main theories in mind Dr. Still began the practice of the therapy he afterwards called osteopathy, and in a few years, with no other method to help him, he made the name of Kirksville, the city of his residence, famous throughout the world, by working out the numerous and seemingly miraculous cures, which the practitioners of his school have been continuing in the years that have followed.

It is clear, however, that the spinal lesion as a cause of disease must be regarded from two points of view, and that two kinds of lesions must be considered. There are what may be called primary lesions—originating in the vertebral column itself, and acting reflexly upon other parts of the body; and lesions secondary in the spine, originating in other parts of the body, and registered in the spine itself—injuries in the spinal tissues, produced, for example, by toxins, the sources of which are remote from the spinal tissues. So, too, there may be in the spine bony lesions—displacements of the vertebrae, or apart from these, and existing without them, certain stiffnesses, tensions, contractures, or other changes in the ligaments and musculature of the spine. It is clear now that if the lesions be primary in the spine their correction should re-establish health. But it is not so clear that the correction of secondary lesions, especially muscle lesions, will be followed

43

by the same results. And in this crux of his work the real genius of Dr. Still is seen. As the very fundamental principle of his theory, therefore, Dr. Still asserted that the blood and the tissues had in them a chemical mechanism that was nature's own prevention and cure of disease. "You do not need drugs," he said. "The blood has a hundred drugs of its own of which the doctor knows nothing. But the body's drugs actually cure the disease, whereas the doctor's drugs kill."

THE BLOOD CONTAINS THE MECHANISM OF HEALING

The lesion in the spine, blocking the free flow of blood to any part of the body, interferes with the chemical conduct of the body, and with the lifting of this embargo nature itself does the necessary work to restore the body to its normal state and even beyond it. Now this principle, as we saw in the first part of our study, is nothing more or less than the first announcement of the general fact of immunity, a principle that has, since Dr. Still's discovery, replaced all other theories of disease and its possible cure.

HUMAN BODY UNDER CONTROL OF OSTEO-PATHIC FINGERS

It has been truly and wisely said that Dr. Still's one grand discovery as a practical therapist was the fact that one human body, with all its wonderful structure and function, with all its marvelous resources and susceptibilities, could be brought under the control of another individual, who, with intelligent understanding of anatomy and the application of the special technique worked out by

Dr. Still, could play upon the mechanism of that body as the skilled performer plays upon the complex musical instrument.

No figure of speech, however, is needed to realize the fact Dr. Still gave to the world a system of therapy absolutely original in every one of its applications; that he at one stroke not only cast aside, in a thorough-going and radical way, the entire system of medical practice with its purges and emetics, its alteratives and demulcents, its anodynes and cholagogues, its stimulants and sedatives, and its thousand and one other superstitions that had fogged the brain and paralyzed the hand of therapy for ages—cleaned out the whole system at one stroke—and replaced it with a practice grounded upon the most striking generalization of physiological science the world has ever known. He gave to the world this entirely new method of treating diseases, the result of which are unparalleled and unapproached in human history. For up to the time of that discovery there was positively no method of treating diseases in general that was followed by any results whatsoever save harmful ones. The only system of therapy at all comparable with osteopathy that has appeared since his time, is that of serum and vaccine therapy, and this has been found to have fallen immeasurably below its first promise and expectation. But serum and vaccine therapy, let it always be remembered, was founded on the identical principle of Dr. Still himself—the body's own natural resistance to disease of every kind. And this therapy is general in no

sense of that word.   So that we can truly say that
osteopathy is the only scientific, universal therapy
as yet put into practice, which in no form whatever depends upon or grows out of any other system or method or theory since men first attempted
the treatment of disease by means other than
those of the medicine man of the savage tribe, who
called in the supernatural to his assistance.

With this absolutely unique and perfectly
original method in their hands, the pupils of Dr.
Still, the men and women trained under his influence, have been treating diseases of every description for twenty years or more, and he would
indeed be a man of neither common sense nor
ordinary fairness nor openness of mind who would
deny the results the profession of osteopathy has
won with no other method than that of what has
been called pure osteopathy by the foremost and
oldest practitioners of the art.   These results have
been culled from thousands of bed-sides and from
tens of thousands of cases pronounced hopeless, or
incurable, by other practitioners of medicine, who
have seen with startled curiosity and vain regret
the osteopathic tide, as it has swept such incurables into the ranks of perfectly healthy men,
women and children. Into all fields and all special-
ties of medicine has osteopathy entered, and each
and every one of the cured incurables has become
in turn a new prophet and propagandist, with
spontaneous testimony as to the virtue of the
method in each particular case.

In this respect, too, osteopathy has differed
most essentially from the two other main special

reforms in medicine. We mean homeopathy and eclecticism—the schools of Hahnemann and Bennett. The great Osler could truly say that the homeopaths, who used virtually no medicine at all, lost as few patients as the old school with poisonous drugs. Indeed they lost fewer. But homeopathy, with its vanishing quantities of drugs, did not cure patients whom the older school dismissed as incurables. And this is precisely what Dr. Still did time and again until his retirement from active life, and what every practitioner of his school has done from the beginning, and is doing every day. These facts form the popular foundation on which the success of osteopathy rests, and this foundation only grows, and can only grow deeper and stronger with the passage of time, as the number of practicing osteopaths increases year by year, and the known results of their practice correspondingly increase.

But the curing of incurables is not by any means the limits of the method, for it must be remembered that the older doctors have been accustomed to confuse the terms "curable" and "recoverable". All diseases from which the patient naturally recovers have been classified as "curable" by the medical profession. But thus far, the diseases that have been cured by the medical art (apart from osteopathic medical art) can be counted on the fingers of one hand.

Dr. Still, going to the heart of the matter, said, in his almost too gigantic way, "I looked around me and asked myself where were the patients we, the doctors, had been treating for disease? And I was compelled to answer, 'They are dead!'—And it was then that I realized that something was wrong with medicine."

It is perfectly safe to say that there never has been a physician from Lieberkuehn to Osler who has not, in his thoughtful moments, felt the same intense conviction that was expressed by Dr. Still in the above words, but the likeness between him and all the others (save four or five) stopped right there. It remained for him to find out what was wrong, to remove the error, and to put in its stead a practical and scientific substitute, and that substitute is osteopathy. What, now, was the error? The answer may be expressed in one word — drugs. And as early as the year 1873 —and earlier—Dr. Still, with one supreme wave of his hand, swept the entire system of drug therapy clear out, root and branch, replacing it with what he called, for want of a better name, Osteopathy. It is difficult for us in these days when osteopathic therapy is one of the established facts of the day to realize the hugeness of Dr. Still's achievement. To realize it fully we must forget what has occurred during the past forty years, place ourselves back with him in 1873, and become conscious of this huge naked fact:

Andrew Taylor Still was not only the originator of manual therapy, but he also (and this is a huger fact) was the originator of drugless medicine!

Drugless medicine is today a fact of universal recognition and force—a fact familiar to the whole world, and perhaps the only forward step that medicine has taken since the time of the ancients; for it is hardly fair to regard the vaccines and the serums of modern times as true drugs, although they are so classified by their users. Nor is it fair to discount the full and sole credit for this great and radical reform which should spontaneously flow to Dr. Still, on the ground that the time was ripe, that drugless medicine was coming anyway, and that if he did not establish it some other man would have done so. Quite true. It would have been established by some other genius of prime order. But the same thing may be said with equal force of all other great reforms whatsoever. Nor yet can we discount that credit by saying that Flaubert, the French physician of the late eighteenth and early nineteenth century, was the first modern to see the vanity and futility of the ancient apothecary system, so well set forth in the realistic novel, Madame Bovary, published about 1850 by his son, Gustave Flaubert, a book that everybody interested in medicine should read. Flaubert's perception was without force and effect, and the entire drug system was absolutely intact afterwards. Nor can we deprive Dr. Still of the entire credit for drugless medicine by saying that the physiologists of the middle nineteenth century were beginning to become convinced that the "remedies" of medicine were in reality poisons— a principle which was afterwards formulated in the pharmacological maxim that all substances that are chemically active in the body are either foods or poisons, and that any substance chemically active in the body that is not a food is therefore a poison.

But what do these facts mean? They mean that Dr. Still's original perception and theory of the action of drugs has been experimentally proved by all the pharmacologists of the world in the past twenty-five or thirty years. We will recur to this matter in a moment. Nor can we classify Hahnemann and Bennett with Still in this respect. For while the great German and the great Scotch reformer of medicine, like the great American reformer, perceived that there was something radically wrong with the medicine of their day, they did no more in the actual practices they founded than substitute one system of drugging for another; the German, indeed, enlarging the number of drugs in use, but reducing the dose to the vanishing point; the Scotchman, on the other hand, increasing the dose by increasing the strength of the drug—the "specific", fresh-extracted drugs of the eclectic. Nor yet can we discount Still's great reform by saying that Virchow, the founder of modern pathology, indirectly demonstrated the futility of drugs by his studies of the tissues of disease, because the lesson that Virchow taught had no practical result against the use of the old remedies, neither in the beginning of his work nor since. Thus if we consider all the elements of reform that were working out the general movement that culminated in the drugless medicine and manual therapy of Still, we will see that his grand generalizations were quite independent of and uninfluenced by these various elements. They were made by a man quite free from all influence of Flaubert, or of Virchow, or of the early physiologists, and of course of Hahnemann and Bennett, for these men were still held fast in the meshes of the drug net. And we can not say that Still was influenced by the researches of pharmacology, for these researches did not become scientifically organized and progressive until long after the drugless manual therapy of Still was a fact familiar to everybody in America.

WHEN DOCTORS DENOUNCED THE PHARMACOLOGISTS

Pharmacology is the science which studies the effects of drugs on the animal body. This science had its beginnings in the experiments which were made by physiologists in the administration of various drugs to animals, principally dogs, and the careful recording of such effects by means of instruments of precision, invented for that purpose. In this way the action of many alkaloids, such as pilocarpin, atropine, strychnine, and others, came to be fully understood, one drug playing the part of antagonist to the other, and the entire effect being recorded on the kymograph—a revolving drum covered with smoked paper on which was written the cure of the blood pressure and respiration. The effects of adrenalin on the blood were demonstrated by this technique, thus suggesting some of the normal effects of the secretion of the adrenal gland in the body. By other and more refined methods of research the effects of nicotine on the nerve centers were brought into view. Also the physiological effects of numerous

drugs, administered freely to their human subjects by physicians, were studied carefully, and
many new perceptions of normal physiology were
thus made by the researchers. But incidentally
was brought out the fact that all drugs were
harmful through the chemical anarchy they produced in the organs of the body.

These investigations and their conclusions were
at first unknown to the medical profession at
large; but when that profession began to understand the meaning of the results of pharmacological science, its members rose up in fierce denunci-
ation of the pharmacologists—charging these gentlemen with drawing conclusions unwarranted by
their experiments, and holding that they had no
business or right to reason from dogs to man—
that because a drug had this or that effect upon
a dog was no reason why it should have the same
effect upon the human body. The doctors saw
that the whole drug therapy was being under-
mined, and that the medical man, deprived of the
use of drugs, would be deprived of the only therapy
he had! Therefore, the medical man fought the
pharmacologists with the same malicious weapon
with which he had long been trying to fight osteopathic treatment and A. T. Still, its discoverer.
But the pharmacologists kept on playing, and
soon a course in pharmacology became an essential
in the up-to-date medical school—a course which
was calculated to leave the medical man at least
partly informed in the effects of the drugs he
would use, did he use drugs at all . And at this
juncture we began to hear, in the medical schools,

much talk concerning "preventive medicine," a medicine drugless quite, but distinctly not therapeutic. What has been the result? The result has been this, that drugs are clear out of court in the general practice of medicine by every well informed and scientifically instructed doctor in America. Treatment has vanished in diagnosis, and the main desideratum of every physician is to find out what it is that ails his patient (the name of the disease), the "treatment" being a wholly problematical matter. In this way has science again confirmed one of the main generalizations of A. T. Still.

HE FIRST PERCEIVED THE TRUTH OF GENERAL IMMUNITY

A fair appreciation of the work that Dr. Still did may be summarized under a few heads.

He was the first to perceive the fact that the animal body had in it, developed by the necessities of the preservation of living forms against obliteration by the destructive agents of disease, and other destructive agents, a natural inherited mechanism of resistance or defense which causes the blood and tissues to react against disease and establish recovery or cure.

He was the first to extend this principle of immunity to virtually all diseases (so called) whatsoever.

He was the first to put into practice the perception that artificially compounded substances called drugs were not only not remedies for disease, but were positively hurtful to the organism, and interferers with the natural mechanism of defense. He was the originator of drugless medicine.

He was the first to found a therapy on mechanical principles, that was calculated to help the body in its efforts to re-establish new physiological equilibriums—new normal states—after disease, in any of its forms, had invaded the body; or when the body was thrown out of its normal action by mechanical (anatomical) lesions.

He was the first to establish a general method of profoundly altering the chemisms of the body (in a way favorable to health and free functioning) by profoundly altering the body's environment, through the use of the hands, in definite manipulations, along the spinal column and its tissues. In other words, he was the first to apply the biological principle of tropisms to an actual therapy, the results of which could not but be good.

These, in brief, were the contributions of A. T. Still to medical science and art, and it is probable that as much can be said for no other man in the history of the medical sciences themselves, when actual practice and results are the things in dispute.

OSTEOPATHY A COMPLEX SYSTEM

If we analyze this system of manual therapy, called osteopathy by its discoverer and protagonist, we shall see that it is by no means the simple thing that so many practitioners of medicine, who have not inquired into its methods and results, have imagined and imagine to this day.

In the first place it is anything but a massage, except in so far as the hands are used in its application. It is based first on natural body resistance to disease, in which must be figured not only the normal histological (and microscopic) anatomy of the body, to say nothing at all of the gross anatomy in which the microscopic structures mass themselves, but also upon the pathological changes (the reactions) that occur in these structures in disease. It is based upon the internal tropisms of the body organism, brought about by the chemistry, or chemisms, of the blood and lymph—a chemism which Dr. Still thrust vigorously forward as his main proposition. It sweeps under its views all the changes that occur in this complex body mechanism because of mechanical faults, whatever their origin, in that gross anatomical structure. It figures the correction of these faults, especially in the spine, as being virtuous in the cure of disease, whether the tissue faults be primary in the spine (or other structure) or secondary in these structures, through the presence of toxins or poisons in the blood, produced and thrown into the blood by the growth of disease germs anywhere in the body. It figures that osteopathic manipulation of the spine, in a theoretically normal state, can and does produce an exaggeration of the body's reaction against the toxins of the body's own activities, an effect the osteopath calls stimulation. But this stimulation not only involves stimulation of organs such as the liver and all other glands, and the involuntary musculature of the body, but stimulation also of those cells that manufacture the antibodies to the germs of disease and their toxins, thus increasing the "antibody content" of the blood, which we may now regard as normal secretions, quite as much as we so regard the gastric juice, the bile, or the products of the internal-secreting organs,— the ductless glands—as normal secretions.

CAUSES THE HUMAN ORGANISM TO PRODUCE ANTI-BODIES

To say that this sort of physiological oil for the body's machinery is simple, is saying more than the barest inquiry into the facts will warrant. A certain widely known writer on internal secretions has said that the osteopath secures his results by stimulating the ductless gland, and this may be so. But until more is known about the ductless glands than is known at present or until it is established that every cell in the body is an individual ductless gland in itself, we can proceed on the theory announced in general terms by Dr. Still himself, that the fingers of the osteopath release the general mechanism of the body against disease in whatever ultimate structure this mechanism may lie, if indeed it lies anywhere in particular. So that we can add another adjective to Dr. Still's idea—that of being general in its principle and application.

In conclusion we can say that the facts of osteopathy, especially in its bearing upon the demonstrable facts of immunity, offers one of the most alluring fields for practical laboratory experiment and we can add, furthermore, that research is not wanting the purpose of which is to

put into the test-tube the results which the osteopath's fingers can work, not only in the human
body but in the bodies of those humbler animals
that have given to biological science the most striking generalizations it has. But such a work would
only put the cap-stone on the grand edifice already
reared by Dr. A. T. Still long before test-tubes or
microscopes were ever dreamed of in this particular way, and not long before science, in the
person of Brown-Sequard, had suggested that in
internal secretion would probably be found the
key to the mysteries of health and disease themselves.

IV

OSTEOPATHY IN THE INFECTIOUS DISEASES

The fact that the blood and the tissues resist diseases of various kinds is one of the most anciently and familiarly known facts of human observation and experience, and it is a fact, furthermore, that has been absolutely demonstrated by the experimental pathologists of Europe and America during the past twenty-five years. This resistance of the blood and the tissues (so called "body resistance") to diseases of every kind—even to those mysteriously caused new growths called "tumors"—has been called immunity by that wonderful group of men in Europe who have done so much to extend the science of the physiology of disease, and to vindicate the theory and practice of Andrew Taylor Still, the founder of osteopathy.

Osteopaths never tire of talking about and referring to Dr. Still, and truly he deserves all praise, as Ehrlich and other great investigators deserve praise for like reasons, namely, their great and original power in seeing deeply into things theoretically; because were it not for theory practice could never become an established fact.

The body cells and the body fluids—that is, blood and lymph—have the power of preventing the growth and multiplication of disease germs and of the cells of which tumors consist. In some persons this so-called "resistance" is absolute. Such persons are perfectly immune to certain diseases. Others are not quite perfectly immune. Others are still less immune (more susceptible), and others still are scarcely immune at all—that is, they are highly susceptible to certain diseases; have scarcely any resistance whatever.

All human beings, however, have a certain amount of resistance to all diseases, and it is this varying amount of resistance to various diseases that lies at the bottom of the whole varying and variable panorama of disease we see in men and in all the lower animals, too; for animals, like men, are bound by the same unvarying natural laws of life and its marvelous chemisms. When it is said that there is a "predisposing cause" of disease, we mean that this body resistance is more or less lacking.

Now, let us consider one other exceedingly important fact: The amount of resistance which any particular individual may have at any particular time, is (as a rule) increased the very moment a disease begins to grow in the body. And this increase of resistance tends to grow with the growth of the disease until the disease conquers the body or the body conquers the disease, or a certain equilibrium is established; and there results a slow "chronic" disease of a certain type. These facts are true in the vast majority of those states of body generally called disease.

This was the original theory of Andrew Taylor Still, announced by him long before the great immunologists of Europe proved it was true by experiments on animals. And it was this very increase of the natural resistance common to all living things that Dr. Still had in mind when he said long ago that the blood and tissues contain in themselves all that is necessary to overcome the disease to which the blood and the tissues are susceptible, providing it is released by adequate adjustment or stimulation.

That is why the osteopath is serene and calm in the conviction of the soundness of his own theory and practice, and indeed the results of osteopathic treatment (wonderful in many cases) are to be accounted for by this explanation and by this explanation alone.

The natural resistance of the body to disease lies in the fact that the blood and the tissues contain countless billions of inconceivably small particles (molecules, in chemical language and, as they were called by Dr. Still, "atoms in the blood"), which have a powerful chemical affinity for the disease germs or their poisons (toxins) or with the cells of tumors, and which, uniting with these germs, toxins, or cells of tumors, neutralize or destroy them, leaving the body sound— what we call "well". These little particles, or molecules, that unite with the substances that produce the symptoms of the disease are called "antibodies", or bodies directed against the agents of the disease. These facts constitute the heart of the great theory of immunity, which, for the past twenty-five years has filled the world with its noise, and which was first suggested and first acted upon in a practical way by Still and his school.

From the above facts it should be clear that any method which can increase the antibodies to disease—which can increase the defenses of the body against disease, which Nature has planted in the body itself—would be a prime and scientific method of treating disease and of producing results which would seem "marvelous" and "miraculous" to persons who did not understand the facts that lie at the root of the phenomenon. Osteopaths have long since grown accustomed to hearing much of their work spoken of as marvelous and miraculous, but few osteopaths are foolish enough to believe that whatever results they have had in the treatment of disease are due to anything but some fundamental law or fact concerning that marvelous mechanism called "the body". The results merely prove the marvel of Nature itself.

INFLUENZA

Not long ago a certain experimenter in a large osteopathic school undertook a series of observations on the results of osteopathic treatment for influenza, and although this work is more interesting for the doctor than for the layman, even the layman can understand something of its important significance.

Almost everybody is familiar with the main facts of influenza. There is first the feeling expressed in the words, "I feel queer today; I don't know what's the matter with me." Next day the symptoms become clearer. There is ache in the back and bones, in the muscles of the neck, back, legs and other parts of the body, pronounced fever, and head, eye and nose symptoms. The "matter" is a "cold" and a "bad" one. And now if the nasal or throat secretions be "smeared" on a bit of glass, stained in a certain way according to the simple technique of bacteriology, and examined in the highest powers of the microscope, countless numbers of a tiny rod-like organism are seen — the bacillus of influenza. They are so numerous that it is plain at a single glance that the nose and throat of the patient are housing and feeding inconceivably vast numbers of this minute organisms, of this bacillus, or "germ", the toxin of which, being absorbed by the tissues and blood, poison the body and produce the symptoms called the grip.

Presently—in a few days—the secretions from the nose and throat are yellowish (pus), and in the pus are still seen many bacilli of influenza, but the number is slowly being cut down; the pus consisting of dead phagocytes—the soldier cells of the blood. The soldier cells and other cells of the body are manufacturing the antibodies (and other substances) which neutralize the toxins, destroy the bacilli, and restore the body to its former normal state. Soon the pus begins to diminish rapidly in quantity, the bacilli of influenza die out and disappear rapidly, and after, say fourteen to twenty-one days, the nasal and throat secretion shows no influenza bacilli at all. The antibodies, produced by the body as a reaction against the germs and their toxin, have worked a "cure". Nature alone has done the job.

If reasonably large doses of quinine be taken (even when the "bowels are kept open" by generous purgatives) this natural "cure" is delayed and the bacilli do not disappear (together with the symptoms) for several days or weeks after Nature, if not interfered with, would have done the job alone. In other words, there is no drug treatment for the grip that does not delay the natural cure.

Now the experimenter in question ascertained certain interesting facts about the grip, which every osteopathic physician understands when he considers the facts about immunity.

If on the second, or even the third day of the infection, a generous and general osteopathic treatment (neck and spine all the way down) be given, so that the spinal nerves are released from tissue tension and well stimulated, there is experienced almost immediately by the patient a most marked relief, something coming so quickly as to be startling; and in some not frequent cases the symptoms during the succeeding twenty-four hours seem to be increased—the patient seems to feel "worse". But before the end of forty-eight hours—sometimes sooner, and sometimes within the twenty-four hours, and without any seeming increase of discomfort — the symptoms almost completely, if not completely disappear. And if the secretions from the nose and throat be now examined only a comparatively few bacilli of influenza are found, and then follows an interesting consequence: The secretion passes into the pus stage several days before it would so pass when Nature is let alone. Observe now a strange fact: If only one such treatment be given, the pus (very small in quantity with very few germs in it), continues to form for some weeks, and in some cases does not finally disappear for two or three months. But if several such treatments be given, say five or six, on successive days, or on alternate days, the pus stage is never reached at all, or, if reached, lasts only a few hours, less than twenty-four in some cases, and the germs disappear from the secretions with almost startling suddenness, the patient remaining entirely without symptoms in the interval.

OSTEOPATHY ABSORBS INFECTIONS

These remarkable facts are known to several osteopaths in practice who have drawn from them only another proof of the old theory on which their practice has been for years based—that osteopathic treatment aborts infection by increasing the natural resistance of the body faster than is the rule with Nature when it is left alone.

But such an abortion of influenza is only a type of the working out of this therapy in infections other than influenza, and we discuss the matter here only to bring before the public one scientific phase of osteopathy out of many.

These facts of influenza—in common with the facts of almost all other diseases—prove that the body has normally a considerable amount of resistance (antibodies) to influenza. Some individuals can not acquire influenza at all—they are perfectly immune, have an excess of anti-influenza bodies in their blood and tissues; others have less, are slightly susceptible to influenza; others are highly susceptible; a few (especially aged persons) have scarcely any resistance at all, and die as a result of their inability to produce the antibodies in sufficient quantity to kill the germs and neutralize the toxins. And there is excellent scientific reason to believe that even many of these aged persons could be saved by osteopathy if treated early in the beginning of the invasion.

All bound up in these facts of immunity is the principle of "vaccines" and their uses in modern therapy and prevention of disease. What are vaccines, how are they used, what success have they had, and how does osteopathic treatment compare with them in results? Also, how does osteopathy compare in its results with the results secured by serum treatment?—for vaccines and serums are two different things, and should not be confused, as they are continually confused in the mind of the layman.

VACCINE EXPERIMENTS

The word "vaccines" has no special reference at all to the practice of vaccination for smallpox. The principle of the two things is precisely the same, but in modern usage when the word "vaccines" is used the "vaccine virus" for the prevention of smallpox is not meant at all. The word "vaccine" and the word "vaccination" were used originally because the virus against small pox was grown in cows. (The Latin word "vacca" means in English "cow.") We can explain the nature of vaccines and serums, whether used for the purpose of curing or preventing disease by discussing influenza in this regard, because what would be true of influenza would be true of any other infection.

If a vaccine cure for influenza were possible, it could be done in this way only: Some of the bacilli of influenza would be taken from the nose or throat of a person infected with a very virulent germ of the disease, and these germs would be grown in what is called a medium by bacteriologists. Each of these minute organisms will divide in two every twenty minutes or so, so that in a short time countless billions of them could be had for use. The germs are easily killed by heat of a certain degree and after killing the germs in that way, they would be suspended in salt solution, and then several millions of the dead bacilli in salt solution could be injected into the blood of the person with influenza. These dead germs would be supposed to do in the body what the toxin from the living ones growing in the patient's nose and throat does—that is, make antibodies faster than the natural infection can make them. In that case the body would be stimulated to increase its resistance in excess of the natural increase, and the reaction would win the day over the living germs already growing in the body. All vaccines are based on this principle; but it should be said that no success whatever has been found in any attempt to make a vaccine for influenza; and the same thing can almost be said with truth for other infections. A vaccine made and administered in this way would have no effect whatever upon influenza, and there is therefore no vaccine cure even claimed for this disease.

A serum for influenza could be made by infecting an animal (horse or sheep) by injections of living influenza germs, or by the injection of the toxins from a culture growth of the germs, and then injecting the serum of the animal into the body of the influenza patient. Such a serum, or such a vaccine could be injected alone, or such a serum and vaccine could be injected simultaneously in the hope of causing the body to react with the production of enough influenza antibodies to cause the disease quickly to disappear. And yet no success at all has been had by such methods with influenza. Theoretically, it is difficult to understand why this is so. Theoretically all infections should yield quickly to vaccines or to serums, or to both; but practically hardly any infections, or other diseases, do actually yield to vaccines or serums. And this in spite of the fact that the animals used for many of these experiments are quite susceptible to the germs employed.

And it should be said that theoretically it is just as hard to understand why influenza and other infections can be and are destroyed by osteopathic treatment. It is possible that stimulation of nerves actually does increase antibodies against disease (once the antibody production has been started by the invasion of the germ), inasmuch as antibody production is virtually a similar process with other body secretions, as those of the stomach, liver, salivary glands, or other glands,

and these secretions are controlled by nerves. The
fact, however, remains that osteopathic treatment
(whether because it adjusts bony lesions, or other
tissue lesions in the backbone, or because it simply stimulates nerves) really and truly aborts and
stops infections, influenza among them. Numerous osteopaths claim (to their fellow practitioners) that their treatment has in numerous
cases stopped typhoid fever, pneumonia, and various other infections, and even the most conservative osteopath will not boldly assert that
any infection is known to be exempt to this peculiar result—the mechanism and the description of
which have been discussed in the first pages of
this paper in our remarks about influenza.

SERUM TESTS TO IDENTIFY VARIOUS DISEASES

The osteopath does not deny the principle on
which serum and vaccine therapy is based, more
than he denies the principle on which are based the
various serum tests for disease, such as the Widal
reaction for typhoid, the Moro and other reactions
for tuberculosis, the Wasserman reaction for
syphilis, the Abderhalden reaction for pregnancy,
the serum test for cancer, the Schick test for
diphtheria antibodies, and other tests of this kind,
which the whole world uses. The osteopath does
not deny the principles on which these tests and
the serum and vaccine therapy are based, because
these principles are his very own, and his own
results are in all probability based on these very
principles themselves, although osteopathic results
have not yet been studied sufficiently to say the
last word upon them. There has as yet been

neither time nor opportunity so to study them. What the osteopath holds is this: that the great principle of immunity has not been found generally successful in the hands of serum and vaccine therapists, whereas that very principle has been found conspicuously successful in the hands of A. T. Still and the physicians whom his principle and therapy have inspired and actuated for at least twenty years in the open daylight of the actual world.

WHEN OSTEOPATHIC LESIONS ARE CAUSED BY TOXINS

What is now to be stated is a fact familiar to every osteopath. If the backbone of a patient suffering with influenza be carefully examined, it will be found that the muscles that house and protect, and that operate the movements of, the individual units of the spine (called vertebrae by anatomists) are tense, stiff and hard, this unusual stress having been brought about by the toxin of the influenza germs; whether this toxin acts directly on the muscles themselves, or upon the muscles through the disturbance in the nervous system caused by the toxin, is indifferent. The fact is, that this backbone muscle-equipment is, in common with other muscles, as in the arms, the legs, the abdomen, the chest, and other parts of the muscular skeleton, made tense and hard, rendering the entire spine comparatively rigid. Now this rigidity in other parts of the body is comparatively unimportant, whereas in the spine it is all-important and critical, because the great nervous mechanism (the spinal cord, and indirectly the brain and the sympathetic nerves, which are connected with the spinal cord by connecting nerve branches—the rami of the anatomists), throws out from between each pair of vertebrae two great trunk nerves, and these numerous trunk nerves supply the entire body with nerve-power; so that all the internal organs, the skin, the bones, the blood vessels, and even the nerves themselves, and the cells of the blood, no doubt, are directly or indirectly, dependent upon these great nerves for their absolute action, even for their minute chemical work. (A pharmacologist of John Hopkins University recently claimed to have proved that the activity and properties of the cells that float in the blood and lymph streams are under control of the nerve impulse.)

A MOVING PICTURE OF THE BODY'S REACTIONS

Here in influenza (and other infections) you have the master-tissue of the body—the nerves —pinched and pressed upon by tissue-tension at its very exit from the great central power house, the spinal cord, and tension there is important. If the osteopath lowers the tension and removes the block by loosening the tissues all along the line from skull to coccyx, we can fairly well account for his quick results in influenza in the following way:

1. The toxin of influenza has entered the blood, and has made rigid (among other muscles) the muscles of the spine.

2. The body cells of the influenza patient are making antibodies as fast as they can.

3. But their work of making antibodies is interferred with, and made slow by the fact that the cells of the body that make the antibodies are dependent upon nerve impulses as stimuli for the work. The more numerous and full the nerve impulses they receive the faster will they function. The less numerous and less powerful the fewer antibodies will they make.

4. If the tissue tension at the exits of the nerves in the spine (tension produced by the toxin) be lowered, the nerve impulses will flow freely to the body cells—to all body cells.

5. This will leave the cells free to make antibodies as fast as they can when not interfered with in any way.

6. But this excess of antibodies quickly neutralizes the toxin and indirectly kills the germs.

7. But this being the case, there is now no longer any toxin to make tense and keep tense the tissues at the exits of the spinal nerves.

8. And thus the entire complex of symptoms of influenza vanishes almost instantaneously, just as if a vast quantity of antibodies had been injected into the blood of the individual at one stroke.

When left alone the work of antibody making is comparatively slow, because normal nerve impulses are partly blocked at the exits of the spinal nerves and the entire normal mechanism of the sympathetic nervous system thrown out.

This theory sounds good and true, and it is the theory upon which the osteopath works in his treatment of many infections.

In these days of popularized science almost every newspaper syndicate and magazine has some writer who tries to interpret the lessons of science in the matter of health to the public, but in none of these have we as yet seen a clear exposition (even for the untechnical public) of the facts of vaccine and serum therapy, such as is given in this present paper, although the writers in question ought to know how to do it, or else cease writing. We could quote instances of the frightful abuse of that kind of therapy by doctors of the theory of antibodies; but what is a sufferer to do when he finds himself advised by doctors who do not know sufficient science to know they are playing with edged tools when they are injecting disease germs (even dead ones) or commercial serums into the bodies of human beings? Fully ninety per cent of the "cures" claimed by medical men for serums and vaccines are absolute folly, as the best bacteriologists and really scientific immunologists (wherever found) will aver upon question. For these latter men have no money interest in the matter. The osteopath, unlike the medical man, does his conscience no violence when he states his claim—which is not that he can cure all the ills of the body, but that he operates on the most soundly scientific bases known, and that his therapy, while founded upon known and proved pathological physiology, in no manner dangerously complicates Nature, causing her to react disastrously because of a fundamental misunderstanding or total ignorance of the peculiar manner in which she jumps.

In the old days before the facts of immunity were so well marked out and studied by the great Ehrlich, Metchnikoff, Bordet and others, "blood poisoning" was a term that was loaded with significance. When "blood poisoning" "set in" hope was abandoned. The term "blood poisoning" is not generally used today but its shadow still hangs over us, and many persons are still frightened when they hear the name. With good cause, too, for blood poisoning is just as bad as it ever was, only now it is called "highly virulent streptococcus septicemia."

When a pathologist uses the word septicemia he understands (or should understand) by that term, bacteria, or disease germs, of any kind in the blood. The term bacteremia is preferred by many. Bacteremia and septicemia mean the same thing. Septicemia of various kinds may be destructive or "dangerous" or deadly, or mild and ultimately harmless, according as the germs or their toxins are virulent and the patient susceptible to the special germ involved. The old "blood poisoning" was later found to be a peculiar germ called streptococcus pyogenes (pus making) of a highly virulent kind universally in the blood and lymph spaces of a person highly susceptible to that peculiar strain of the germ. Death is almost certain in such a case. Now, if some of the germs could be taken from the body of such a patient, grown, killed and injected within twenty-four hours, the patient might (theoretically) be saved by the excess of antibodies liberated by the presence in the body of the excess of the germs themselves. But this can not be done. Sufficient germs can not be grown in time to save the life of the person infected. The germs throw out a toxin so powerful and diffusible that the individual's vital tissues are destroyed beyond recovery in forty-eight hours. And yet there is a man in London who claims he saves cases of this kind by this vaccine method right along in forty-eight hours. The world's bacteriologists will not believe him. It is hard to understand how it can be done. Nobody can repeat him. We have no record that any osteopath has ever treated a case of that kind, but certainly if such a patient would early secure an osteopath, on the principle that the osteopath could at least "do no harm," another infection (and an essentially wicked one) might be added to the growing list of infections which of late years have been coming more and more under osteopathic dominion.

SCARLET FEVER AND OTHER INFECTIOUS DISEASES

One of the main obstacles that has helped to bar the way of osteopathic success has been the timidity of patients to enlist the services of the osteopathic doctor in diseases such as scarlet fever, infantile paralysis, smallpox, "blood poisoning" of the virulent type, as well as other septicemic pus-forming infections, such as those due to colon bacillus, staphylococcus pyogenes aureus, or even the gonorrheal germ, which causes arthritis (inflammation of the joints) and heart insufficiency. These infections, even when developed, have been palliated by osteopathic treatment, nor

74

do we know to what extent completely removed. Chronic boils and pustulating pimples are a legitimate field for osteopathic treatment, the principle in all these infections being identical with the principle laid down in our discussion of influenza at the beginning of this paper.

"Doctor," you will ask, "do you claim that osteopathy can cure all these diseases?"

DIPHTHERIA ACCORDING TO OSTEOPATHIC TRADITION

Our answer is rational and fair. It is this: Of these infectious diseases we claim that we can cure vastly more cases—that we actually do cure vastly more cases than are cured by vaccine therapy, which can be counted upon only in the smallest number of cases. As for the serum therapy, it may be said that no infection has been found at all amendable to serum treatment save diphtheria alone, and as far as diphtheria is concerned it should be said that osteopathic tradition from the beginning has claimed to be able to cure diphtheria, and that numerous osteopaths positively refuse to use the diphtheria antitoxin, and prefer to rely on osteopathy alone, even when the patients are their own children.

V

OSTEOPATHY IN INFLAMMATORY DISEASES

To Dr. A. T. Still, founder of osteopathy, belongs much if not most of the credit for the modern recognition of the fact that inflammations are, in reality, not diseases in themselves, but the results of the body's attempt to kill and cast out the harmful germs which, when they enter the body that is not sufficiently protected against them, produce what has been called "disease". In the preceding chapter we discussed the nature, effects and causes of infectious diseases, and related how osteopathy can and does not only change and relieve these diseases, but also cures them— that is, reduces their active effects to zero.

In former times inflammations were themselves regarded as diseases, and naturally enough, when one considers how very little was known concerning them. All true inflammations consist, according to the ancient definition of these peculiar changes in the tissues, of redness, swelling, heat and a certain amount of pain or discomfort. These were regarded as the "four cardinal signs" of an inflammation. The inflamed part became red, it was swollen as compared with the normal state, it was hotter (fever) than in the normal state, and there was always pain—great or small as the case may be. Now in so far as the inflammation was regarded as a disease—the effort of the old style medicine (the healing art) was naturally directed against the inflammation (not against the cause of it)—it was deemed desirable to stop the inflammation or "reduce" it, at the same time reducing the fever that accompanied it. It had been found that if blood in generous quantities be withdrawn from the veins, the fever in a diseased body would be reduced. Therefore, it was believed that bleeding was a good remedy against inflammation and it was commonly practiced by all the old doctors. The professors of the healing art gave up their old method of bleeding only after a most bitter fight. But even after exhaustively bleeding the patient had been abandoned as a therapy, it was still believed that it was the inflammation that constituted the essentials of the disease. In recent years, however, this belief has vanished, and the intelligent doctor of today knows that an inflammation, wherever found, is only the reaction of the body against the invading germs, or other destructive agents.

WHY INFLAMMATION CAUSES PAIN

Why? Because inflammation primarily consists of an unusual quantity of blood being drawn to the part. Hence, the heat, the swelling, the redness and the pain; for the unusual swelling of the inflamed part causes pressure on the delicate nerve endings in the part, and this pressure causes pain.

Now when this unusual quantity of blood in the engorged and enlarged blood vessels of the part flows back into the general circulation, and the lymph that has exuded from the engorged blood vessels into the tissues of the inflamed part flows out into the lymph vessels—all signs of the inflammation disappear and the part has been restored to its normal condition.

Nature accomplishes this reaction in ways peculiar to the peculiar pathogenic germ that is causing the trouble. Sometimes pus is formed, as in boils or carbuncles; sometimes fibrin is formed, as in pneumonia, diphtheria, and other fibrin-forming inflammations; but whatever the peculiar reaction may be, it is always based on the principle that the blood and the cells of the blood and of other tissues aim first to conteract, destroy and remove the direct causes that are destroying the tissues. And when this has been done, repair of the destroyed parts naturally follows. All these facts are now well known to pathologists, but such knowledge is of comparatively recent growth, and there is no therapy that is based on these facts so firmly and scientifically as osteopathy.

DR. STILL EARLY PERCEIVED THAT THE BLOOD CURES

To A. T. Still belongs the credit for having been one of the first, if not the very first, to perceive the great natural laws that underlie the facts as we write them. For what was Dr. Still's argument? It was this: Nature to cure the "disease" sent blood in unusual quantity to the part, thus producing an inflammation. When, now, the cure had been worked out by the inflammation, the symptoms subsided (that is the inflammation) and the tissue became nearer normal, if not quite so. But since this is nature's own way of curing, the use of any method which would send blood into the part, in greater quantity than nature itself could send it into the part, would assist nature and hasten the cure, or actually initiate a cure, where, if left alone, nature would never of itself be capable of sending in enough blood to do the business, with disaster or death in prospect as a consequence.

Osteopathy, therefore, teaches that an inflammation is nature's own method of curing certain diseases called infections; and it further teaches that by artificially increasing the quantity of blood flowing into an infected place, natural results can be obtained in greater quantity, and much more quickly, than unassisted nature herself can obtain them. This teaching, from the standpoint of pure science, as this subject has been illuminated in recent years, is scientifically unassailable—and it works!

But osteopathy does more than increase the inflammatory reaction of the blood in infections. We say that it must do more, otherwise there could be no really scientific way of accounting for the peculiar results which are the common experience of osteopathic treatment in certain infectious diseases as the grip, pneumonia and typhoid fever, when the poisons (toxins) made by the germs are diffused throughout all the circulation, and hence through all the tissues of the body.

Let us glance at a common infection that produces an inflammation typical of the pathogenic germ involved, and also typical of the location in the body where the germs are growing. This infection is known as furuncle or in common language boils. What is a boil? It used to be believed by the old doctors (and is still believed by the uniformed) that boils were an indication of "impurity of the blood" and that this "badness" or "impurity of the blood", was "coming out" in the boils. Hence the old school of drug doctors had certain "remedies" not only for boils but for all other eruptions on the skin, especially eruptions that had pus in them, and these remedies were called by the old doctors "depurants" or remedies that cleared the blood of pus (such as sarsaparilla or other "purifiers").

THERE IS NO PUS IN THE BLOOD

In the word "depurant" the syllable "pur" is the same word as "pus", so that depurants depusified the blood—took the pus out of the blood, according to this delusion. The theory was that the pus which came out was originally in the blood, else it could not come out! Now there is no pus in the bood, but there are certainly in the blood many millions of white cells which, when they increase in number and gather by the millions in some certain place, and are killed by the disease germs, which they take into themselves to rid the body of them and their poisons, form pus. Pus in reality consists chiefly of the dead white cells (the leucocytes, phagocytes) that have lost their lives in defending the body from the invading germs. An inflammation that forms pus is called a purulent inflammation; and a boil, or furuncle, as it is called by the pathologists, is one type of purulent inflammation presenting phases, or characters, peculiar to itself because of the place where it is growing, that is, in the skin. Boils are caused directly by the presence in the deep part of the skin, or under the skin, of a germ called staphylococcus pyogenes aureus—staphylococcus, because the little spherical germs grow in the form of bunches; pyogenes because this germ draws to the neighborhood in which it is multiplying the white cells of the blood that when dead form pus; and aureus because the colonies of the germ, when grown in pure cultures outside the body on a medium such as gelatin, or agar, in a test tube or other vessel, are golden in color, aureus meaning "golden" and nothing else. There are several different varieties of staphylococci, but this particular one is the most commonly concerned. Now this germ enters the body by passing down the microscopic space surrounding a hair. The individual germs are so small as to be distinctly visible only under very high powers of the microscope, say a magnification of about 1,000 diameters of the object itself. The individual germ is scarcely larger than about 1-25000 of an inch—a size so small as to surpass the power of the imagination. It can therefore have an easy passage in the smallest crevices, or chinks, or holes in the skin, and it actually makes its way into the deeper parts of the skin in this way.

Once in it finds itself surrounded by the richly nourishing fluid that nourishes the skin—the so called lymph of the body, that passes out through the walls of the tiny capillaries that convey the blood to the remotest corners of the tissues. Here the germ finds a "medium" of growth and nourishment finer and richer than any artificial medium the bacteriologist can make in his laboratory, and the staphylococcus begins to multiply! In multiplying it throws off from its inconceivably minute body the excretions of its life growth, and these excretions are poisonous to the tissues. But they do not diffuse easily, so that the area of infection is more or less limited to the locality of the original entrance point. The tissue cells die and digest themselves, and the liquid substance produced by the auto-digestion diffuses around the place to the nearest blood vessels and attracts to the vicinity the white cells which, when they arrive at the spot where the germs are multiplying, ingest or engulf the bacteria and are killed by the germs. But the germs themselves are killed in their own turn by the white cells and in this way the pus is formed.

HOW A BOIL IS CAUSED

Meanwhile, the poisonous substances made by the bacteria and the dying tissues have caused a powerful flow of blood to the part, by causing the calibre of the little vessels to open out wide, letting in the blood by simple mechanical law of hydrostatics, so that previously to the pus formation the part becomes highly swollen, red and hot—in other words inflamed, and down through the center of the inflamed area is a plug of yellowish solid material, the "core" of the boil. This core consists of dead skin tissue, not yet all dissolved, filled with white-yellowish pus cells. The boil may "break" out on the surface of the skin—if the inflammation be rapidly formed—and with this release of the pus the germs are also carried out of the pocket and the injury heals rapidly leaving only a slight scar. If the development of the inflammation be slower, however, the "core" is formed, the subsequent repair is slower also, and the scar will be larger and deeper. But it is clear from what has been said that the more rapidly formed the inflammation, the more rapid will be the healing process. And the rapidity of the entire proceeding will be determined largely by the quantity of blood drawn to the part in the beginning of the infection.

Now if osteopathic treatment be given for a boil at the beginning of the inflammation, the excessive quantity of blood, over and above the natural quantity which is sent into the part by the treatment, will hasten the inflammation in an artificial way, and hence such an infection can be shortened in its course by just that much. And this has occurred in the treatment of boils by osteopathy.

HOW THE BLOOD WORKS ITS CURE

We can partly explain these interesting facts in this way: A certain amount of blood is needed to neutralize the poisons and destroy the life of a certain number of germs in the tissues. If these germs did not multiply in number a given quan-

tity of blood would do the work in a given time.
But the number of germs is constantly growing,
and inasmuch as nature itself can supply only a
limited amount of blood in a given time, the inflammation must grow larger as the number of
germs increase, and it must grow larger at a
higher rate than the rate at which the number of
germs grows; else the multiplication of the germs
could never be stopped. The entire time required
by nature to do the work is generally—when the
germs are growing in the skin—about ten days;
after which the inflammation subsides because the
germs have been almost all killed. But it can be
seen that if the rate at which the blood flows into
the part be increased beyond the natural rate, the
inflammation, just because it is increased out of
its natural proportion, should be correspondingly
shortened; and this is the actual fact.

But it would appear from this that there must
be something in the blood that kills the germs.
What is this thing?

To answer this question we must direct the attention of the reader to certain substances in the
blood called opsonins by their discoverer, Sir Almroth E. Wright, of London. Opsonins are substances in the blood which have a chemical affinity
for bacteria—the germs of disease—including
staphylococcus pyogenes aureus. These substances unite with the bacteria so that the white
cells can engulf them, thus killing them and removing them from the tissues and forming pus.
If the blood of an individual be rich in the opsonin
against this particular germ that causes boils, the

few germs that enter the skin, or under it, are at once changed by their union with this special opsonin and the bacteria are now engulfed by the leucocytes.

The presence in the blood of these peculiar substances called opsonins, and their action in the way described, constitutes the immunity of the individual against the special germs against which the opsonins are directed. Upon these facts is based the great phagocytic theory of immunity, originated by the late Professor Elie Metchnikoff, of Paris, who died recently, and who has always been regarded by osteopaths with a certain reverence as having in a considerable degree explained by scientific experiments the remarkable effects of osteopathic treatment in certain infectious diseases. Osteopaths have also had much repect and admiration for Sir Almroth E. Wright, the Englishman who discovered and proved the presence in the blood of the opsonins, and thus entirely vindicated the original work of the great and powerful Metchnikoff. For the osteopath can see clearly how a local infection such as boils, if we assume the presence in the blood of the opsonin bodies (which are as truly "antibodies" as are the other antibodies so widely discussed today), can be abated and cured by causing the blood in larger quantities (and hence the opsonins in the larger quantities) to flow through the infected part.

There is another interesting fact about the results of osteopathic treatment in the case of boils, when the osteopathic doctor attacks this disease in time, that is, early after the appearance of the first redness and swelling.

Almost invariably whenever a boil appears it is followed by several new ones. Boils as a general rule come in crops. Why is this the fact? Because when the germ-containing pus breaks out on the skin, the germs are smeared over the unaffected skin, and some of these germs, being still alive and virulent, make their way into the skin, or under it, through the spaces alongside of the hairs of the skin—just a repetition of the original infection. This spread of the infection will go on until the skin, all around the original site of the infection, has become immune by the natural production of the anti-staphylococcic opsonin. The entire infection will now clear up—if the individual's body can make the opsonin in sufficient quantity. When the reverse is true we have what is called "Chronic boils".

WHY OSTEOPATHY PREVENTS A SECOND CROP

But if the patient has had osteopathic treatment in time, if blood has been thrown in liberal quantities into the part, the excess of the specific opsonin thrown into the blood causes, apparently, a certain peculiar change in the germs by which they are rendered less virulent, or more easily and quickly engulfed by the soldier cells of the blood, and hence when the original boil breaks, and these germs now enter the skin alongside the hairs, the germs are quickly disposed of by the phagocytes of Metchnikoff, and no second boil appears. The infection does not spread. These things occur also when the patient, for one or another reason, has been taking osteopathic treatment, and becomes infected by this peculiar germ. Only one boil appears and its course is quickly and mildly run, with comparatively little pain and no reinfection. Only one explanation of these peculiar facts can be given, and that is that osteopathic treatment not only makes full use of the quantity of opsonin naturally in the body, but also actually increases the total quantity of this opsonin naturally circulating in the blood.

HEALTHFUL BLOOD NATURE'S BEST GERMICIDE

Now this is the very result which Sir Almroth E. Wright has attempted to produce by his so-called vaccines, or dead staphylococci, which he injects into the blood of the patient suffering with boils, after having grown them from germs taken from the patient's own lesions. The world's bacteriologists and immunologists all agree in the verdict that Wright's claims must be exaggerated, for no one but Wright himself has been able to secure the results claimed by him. It is highly significant that osteopathy here, as elsewhere in the infectious diseases, seems quite competent to do the very things which the vaccine therapy theoretically should be able to do and cannot. It is not to be argued from this that Sir Almroth E. Wright is wrong in his experiments with the opsonins, for he certainly has made a prime discovery which, theoretically should be able to work cures in infections from these peculiar germs, but which fails in all but a comparatively few cases.

87

Neither Wright nor any other scientific investigator (outside of the osteopaths) has tried the effect on the work of opsonins by flushing the parts with larger quantities of natural blood than the normal inflammation contains. Osteopathy, by washing the inflamed part with increasing streams of normal blood actually brings larger supplies of normal opsonin to the part than could possibly flow to it normally; but it is also more than probable that the total amount of this antibody is increased by the treatment.

VIRULENT TONSILLITIS

Somewhat similar phenomena appear when virulent tonsillitis is treated at the beginning of the infection by thorough osteopathic manipulation. That the virulence of bacteria (germs) can be sensibly lessened, and even quite destroyed, by osteopathic treatment, need not be doubted today; and the time is not far away when scientific research will clear up much of the mystery that now puzzles osteopaths in the results they secure in the treatment of infectious diseases.

Tonsillitis in varying degrees of virulence can be caused by several entirely different germs, but typical painfully virulent tonsillitis, accompanied by systemic fever, is nearly always (la grippe aside) due to the growth in the tonsils of a pus-making germ called streptococcus pyogenes (streptococcus because the germs grow in the form of chains).

Not long ago a culture of streptococcus pyogenes was made from the throat of a child who had an intense inflammation of the tonsil accompanied by high temperature. The parents of the child had called in an osteopath at the very first appearance of the attack. The temperature (fever) was marked and the tonsil typical. But the osteopath (fortunately for the child if unfortunately for the experiment) had given the patient two thorough treatments before taking the "swab" from the throat. After the first treatment the fever had reduced almost to normal, and after the subsequent treatment the tonsils had been distinctly relieved and the fever almost all removed. The germs were still there in quantity, but when their virulence was tried out in a laboratory experiment, the germs were found to be quite harmless. Now it is only rational to conclude that the treatment had directly to do with the destruction of the virulence of this germ, for such a tonsillitis —if let alone—would normally run its usual course, and recovery take place only after the body had immunized itself against the germ by an increase in the anti-streptococcic bodies in the blood. Theoretically a vaccine should do what this osteopath did, but practically such a result is rare in vaccine therapy. The laws underlying these remarkable results of osteopathic treatment will certainly some day be established by scientific osteopathic research, but in the meantime the osteopathic practitioner can, in the interest of his patients, assume that his own theory of results is ample to account for them, and go on treating infectious diseases in the proved conviction that his peculiar form of mechano-therapy as worked out by Dr. A. T. Still actually and practically does what serum and vaccine therapy should invariably do but unfortunately does not.

One of the most remarkable results in the osteopathic treatment of infections, familiar from of old to all practitioners and even students of this art, is the result in acute and chronic dysentery. Dysentery (diarrhoea) is most frequently caused by the growth in the intestine of one of the several types of germs producing the typical flux from the intestine. Pressure on the spine (in a way peculiar to osteopathic theory and practice) quickly stops dysentery when caused by these germs. The treatment is familiarly known to osteopathic doctors as "inhibition". Dr. A. T. Still early demonstrated the entire curability of dysentery by this method in quickly restoring to normal a number of children afflicted in this way. His early success has been followed up ever since that time by the members of his school who have come to regard this kind of dysentery as a simple matter for the osteopath to cure.

DRUGS DO NOT ACT LIKE OSTEOPATHY

What is the drug treatment for dysentery? There are two methods opposite in theory and practice. One is to clean out the intestine with a purgative, the other is to paralyze the intestine by drugs such as chloroform. Capsicum (red pepper) and chloroform will often suddenly stop the movement of the intestines in dysentery, but never as quickly as osteopathic inhibition. The chloroform may act as an inhibition of the growth of the germs, but this inhibition is not at all what is meant by the osteopath when he uses that word. Osteopathic inhibition is temporary stoppage of the movement of the intestine, and this stoppage is entirely free from the after effect which follows the use of the drug. Permanent recovery quickly ensues, and in some way the multiplication of the germs in the intestine is stopped. Possibly this growth is stopped by the accumulation of their own secretion products in the intestine, but more probably by the production in the blood of the intestines of substances that escaping into the intestines do the damage to the germs there. It is difficult to account for the results of osteopathic treatment in dysentery unless some back bone lesion is assumed to exist even where it is invisible; but the certainty of the results is one of the most remarkable and interesting of the innumerable interesting facts of the osteopathic therapy.

INCREASING THE BODY'S RESISTANCE

When we say that osteopathic treatment reduces the virulence of disease germs, we can only mean one thing, and that is that osteopathic treatment increases the body's resistance to the germs in question once the germs are in and multiplying. No definite experimental proof has ever been established that the body's resistance to disease germs can be increased by osteopathic treatment before an infection is introduced into the body. That is to say, it has not yet been experimentally proved that osteopathic treatment can so increase the body's resistance to all germs that this treatment can be absolutely regarded as a preventative of infection, as for example when vaccine for typhoid fever prevents the individual treated from acquiring typhoid fever. And yet, pending such experimental evidence, the osteopath is warranted in assuming that general osteopathic treatment actually does accomplish some such body change, for we know as a matter of fact that osteopathic treatment vastly increases those normal reactions of the body which are, in fundamental physiology, physiologically similar to the body's reactions against infectious germs and their toxins.

WHY OSTEOPATHY REFRESHES AFTER FATIGUE

For example, an osteopathic treatment when one is tired and exhausted after a day's hard work will wonderfully refresh the body and restore its vigor, producing a physiological reaction very nearly equivalent to a good night's sleep. This is a fact familiar to all osteopaths, many of whom are eager to get such a treatment for themselves whenever a friendly fellow practitioner is near by and agreeable. Now what does this reaction mean? If it means anything it means that the osteopathic manipulation of the spine actually does what sleep will do for a similarly tired man. And sleep, it is known, refreshes and strengthens the body in all its parts, and in all its cells, by neutralizing the poisons released by the work of the body's cells in their activities during the waking state. The nerve cells, the muscle cells and all the other cells (but principally these two master tissues) work, and in working throw out of themselves into the blood stream certain chemical waste substances which react on the nerve cells as toxins—the toxins of fatigue. During sleep the body cells manufacture antibodies that neutralize the fatigue toxins, and the nerve cells therefore feel fresh again. Simple feeding of the nerve cells is not sufficient. These fatigue substances must be neutralized and several hours are necessary to do it—hours during which no further fatigue toxins are made by muscle and nerve. But osteopathic treatment will encompass after 30 minutes what otherwise requires several hours of sleep. Thus does osteopathic treatment stimulate the body to the rapid production of antibodies against normal toxins made by the normal activities of the normal boy's cells.

Now the toxins of disease are toxins not made by the body's own cells, but by the foreign cells called disease germs, and it is reasonable to say that the effect of osteopathic treatment on the normally tired body is regulated by the same physiological law that underlies the production of antibodies to the toxins of disease.

VI

OSTEOPATHY IN THE GROUP OF SO-CALLED RHEUMATIC DISEASES

Rheumatism is a disease as old as history, and in ancient times men resorted to mineral springs for the relief of the pains, the twinges, the swellings, the soreness, the sudden sharp stabs, the acute disabling inflammation, the chronic pain and deformity—all of which were lumped together in the ancient medical mind and labeled in gross rheumatismus. Perhaps under no one name have so many widely divergent and radically different disorders been classified as under this old term rheumatism.

NEARLY ALL PAINS ONCE CALLED RHEUMATIC

Until yesterday one may say, "rheumatism" was perhaps the most mysterious of diseases that tortured with strong pain or only just annoyed its victim. For in this many-headed disease all degrees of symptoms were recorded, from the smallest, most insignificant "pain" in the end of the toe or finger, which came and vanished so quickly that the individual could not be certain it was there at all, to long drawn out chronic torture that inflamed, enlarged and deformed the joints of the body with such racking and exhausting pain that one might well wonder how the victim could remain sane in mind.

94

"Rheumatism," as this panorama of pain was called from of old, was studied in modern times by the best physiologists, bacteriologists and pathologists in the world without result. It was believed to be due to some chemical disturbance or unbalance in the body in which uric acid, or lactic acid, or some other acid, was not destroyed in the body, or was poorly eliminated, as is the known case with uric acid in gout. But this theory was long ago abandoned. It was believed to be due to diet, but no proof of this belief was ever brought forward. It was more recently believed to be due to the growth in the body of a microscopic germ, called by the man who believed he had found it, micrococcus rheumaticus. But bacteriologists in general were never convinced that this particular germ was the cause of rheumatism. The mystery of rheumatism promised never to be solved, and so it was that the old name lingered, and the doctors continue to prescribe anodynes, that is, drugs that that dulled pain—opiates—not because the anodynes could cure or were believed to cure rheumatism, but because so-called rheumatism was accompanied by pain, and anodynes would dull pain of any kind. Dosing the "rheumatic" patient with anodynes—or pain killers—helped to kill the patient, to ruin the heart, to make the suffer suffer more. And so the use of anodynes in rheumatism came to be regarded as dangerous, and the wise doctor, for the patient's own good preferred to allow the rheumatic person to suffer rather than to risk killing him with drugs.

95

But the mystery of rheumatism has been recently and finally cleared up by the discovery—which has been for several years dawning on the scientific mind—that what has been called rheumatism is not one single disease, that is, a disease due to one unvarying cause, but a great number of symptoms caused by several different causes, the one thing common to all being the various kinds of pain. Until very recently we used to classify rheumatism into several kinds—inflammatory rheumatism (rheumatism accompanied by inflammation) ; rheumatoid arthritis (which was an inflammation of the joints milder than articular rheumatism or "like" rheumatic joints) ; articular rheumatism (in which the joints were swollen and the pain intense) ; muscular rheumatism (when the pain was in the muscles) ; neuralgic rheumatism (in which the pain was dull, chronic and distinctly of the tooth-ache variety) ; rheumatic neuralgia (in which the pain was like that of the no less mysterious neuralgia, mixed with rheumatic signs) ; neuritis (which resembled rheumatism but was different in some ways) ; sciatica (pain in the great sciatic region) ; lumbago (pain in the lumbar region of the back) ; certain symptoms of the heart (called rheumatism of the heart) ; similarly of the stomach, and so on, without end.

Only a short time ago, it was believed that rheumatism was caused by the entrance into the body of some mysterious germ thru the tonsils; and forthwith it became the fashion for people to have their tonsils removed (by a rather bloody and distressing if simple surgical operation). But even this last stand on the old ignorant basis has now been abandoned, and it has been seen that while one of the troubles that was labeled rheumatism can and does come in by way of the tonsil, removing uninfected tonsils is a rather crude, hit-and-miss way of preventing disease; is rather, an excellent method of inviting other and worse disasters by taking away the natural fortifications of the body against invading organisms of many kinds.

How, then, let us ask, has the mystery been cleared up, and if there is no such thing in reality as rheumatism, what is the nature of the many different things that produce in the body the various aches and pains, swellings and tortures, twinches and "touches" that have been all along thrown together and labeled rheumatism from time out of mind?

WHEN DUE TO ANATOMICAL MAL-ADJUSTMENTS

The osteopathic practitioner of five or ten or twenty years experience will understand much of the mystery when he thinks in retrospect of the persistent "rheumatisms" he has cured—occasionally with a single treatment. Well does such an osteopathic practitioner know, and well has he known for years, that an enormously large proportion of the "rheumatism" going the rounds of the human race was and is anything but mysterious, at least in its cause; for every such a practitioner has seen many cases of "rheumatism"—cases that would be labeled such by all the doctors in the world—which were caused by a ridiculously simple slip or misplacement or strain in some joint or tissue, the results of which were not always so simple as the cause. Such cases vary from long continued—nearly incessant—pain in a hand, a foot, an entire arm or leg, in both arms or legs, in the breast, in the entire upper part of the body, or in the entire lower part—from such a pain, we say, to intermittent stabbings and shootings of pain, which, like the true old "rheumatics" come and go with the weather and without it. But give the required adjustment, and such rheumatism is gone for good.

It is quite impossible to say what percentage of "rheumatisms" are caused by just such lesions. It is likewise impossible to say how many cases of neuritis, in which the entire upper body, the trunk, or large areas of it, are due, if not to bony lesions in the back, then to hardened and tense muscles along the spine, for the osteopath is familiar with such cases also, and has removed the ill permanently by loosening up the joint-binding tissues of the spine.

Here, then, is one great source of many of the pain-complexes known in the past as rheumatism—anatomical disturbances, often minute in their nature. Let us illustrate.

INTERCOSTAL NEURALGIA

The wife of a certain well known national statesman had "rheumatism" in the breast and arms for years—rheumatism it was called by some; a kind of neuralgia by others; a neuritis by others; and some of her many doctors had reservations in their minds that it might be that peculiar thing called angina pectoris, or, in common English, "breast-pang". She finally came into the hands of an osteopath who found a twisted rib which was plainly to be seen on a front view, or distinctly felt by drawing the fingers across the side of the chest. The cure was made by adjusting the rib into line with its fellows, and the mysterious "rheumatism" of years standing vanished, and never recurred. You can not blame this lady for being a "comfirmed believer" in osteopathy, can you?

BRACHIAL NEURITIS

A young man for years was partially disabled by pain in the right arm—pain that came and went suddenly, that gave him token of changes in the weather (at least so he himself was convinced), and pain that was clearly rheumatic. Also pain that was clearly a "neuritis" and was so diagnosed time and again. He was a portly man and a good liver, and he was for many years a victim of the diet regimen—starving himself to get the "poisons" out of his system. An osteopath found one of his ribs out of joint—had been out of joint for years—and slipped it back into its proper adjustment. Cure—perfect.

PROMISCUOUS TONSIL SLAUGHTER

A form of "rheumatism" much more common than is generally supposed, called bursitis when its nature has been recognized by osteopaths, consists of pain in or near a joint and extending down the limb, as pain in one of the shoulders,

with involvement of the arm, often accompanied
by sensations of numbness in the arm and fingers.
Bursitis is an inflammation of a bursa, or tissue
pad found in the joints—a kind of water cushion
for the joint. This inflammation can be caused
by physical strain from accident and is due in a
vast majority of cases to some such accidental
wrench or strain, as described. During the past
few years several osteopaths who were themselves
almost disabled by such "rheumatisms" have been
perfectly restored by osteopathic treatment, and
today such cases are almost invariably not only
relieved but absolutely cured by making proper
adjustments. Until osteopathy was found available in these cases the only remedy was the surgeon's knife, by which the bursa itself was removed, thus leaving the arm more or less disabled. Shoulder and arm "rheumatisms", persistent in their character, are frequently found to
be due to this so-called bursitis which in all probability is not caused at all by disease germs but
by simple mechanical tissue lesions.

A DISABLED ARCH OF THE FOOT

Another similar simple example was found in
an elderly lady who for years suffered with "rheumatic pains" in her foot. Once, long ago, she had
turned a bone in her instep, and the joint, as is
common in such cases, would slip in and out with
stress in walking. The rheumatism would "come
and go suddenly as by magic", to use the phrase
of the "confirmed rheumatic". She had avoided
red meats, acid foods, and other supposed aggra-

vators of the rheumatic tendency for years, and to no purpose. An osteopath was found who understood the sources of the pain, and subsequently would invariably "cure" the rheumatic attack by a simple deft rotation of the joint.

SCIATICA FROM A SLIPPED PELVIS

Another case was that of a professional man who for many years had been tortured with severe "sciatic rheumatism" and who had gone the "usual round of the doctors", and was cured in the usual way—by osteopathy. It was found that this man had a twisted pelvis, which, when it had been "twisted" back again into its normal bony relations, by osteopathic technique, was seen to be the cause of the entire trouble. Such instances could be multiplied many times over with as many variations according to the determination of the dislocation, the stress, the tensity of the tissues involved, in various parts of the body, every osteopath being able to cite numerous cases of his own, in which his own experience has taught him that these anatomical causes lie at the root of innumerable examples of that great pathological octopus labeled in the museum of disease as rheumatism. This patient had long worn red flannel undergarments, summer and winter, in the belief that the conservation of his body heat would relieve him of his pain, and had resorted to the use of various drugs and other remedies, and hygienic measures in general, but of course could get no help from such methods of treatment as long as the lesion in the pelvis was there to disturb the normal relations of the great nerve and the tissues it supplied.

Another form of pain, commonly called rheumatism, and most often neuritis, is caused by slight displacement of one of the vertebrae of the neck—frequently that next to the skull itself. The slight pressure resulting gives the patient a chronic "headache", or neuralgia", the real cause of which is not always recognized. But if the case is carefully studied and the lesion reasoned out, its correction is reasonably sure, and adjustment of the bone back into its normal bearing will cause the pain to disappear, with what relief to the patient those who have suffered or are suffering in this way, can easily imagine.

But there are causes of "rheumatism" other than imperfect articulations or hardened tissues. and here, too, the osteopath has a method of rational therapy unique and helpful, more so than any other known method, altho these other causes are more strictly classifiable as diseases. We refer to pain called rheumatic, or neuritic, or neuralgic, that are caused by disease germs, or their poisons, in the blood and the tissues or by so-called auto-intoxications, which will give one "rheumatic" twinges and sharp pains in any or in all parts of the body.

INFECTIOUS VARIETIES OF "RHEUMATISM"

To these classes of rheumatisms belongs that severe and most striking disease called articular rheumatism which is frequently followed by heart lesions more or less serious according as the disease germ is highly or mildly virulent and the patient's blood and tissues susceptible to the germ in high or low degree.

It was in such cases of intensely painful "articular rheumatism" that the bacteriologists sought for their causative germ, with the discovery, or what was thought to be the discovery, of the micrococcus rheumaticus. The cause of this disease is now definitely known, and it is a germ mentioned in former numbers of this magazine, namely, streptococcus pyogenes, the same germ that causes virulent tonsillitis, inflammation of the valves and muscle wall of the heart, abscesses in various parts of the body, erysipelas, and that deadly thing called "blood poisoning" of the most virulent type.

INFLAMMATORY "RHEUMATISM"

In rheumatism of this kind the germ finds lodgment perhaps in the tonsil, and from the tonsil works its way into the blood and becomes what pathologists and bacteriologists call a "septicemia". Reaching the joints, the germs grow in the fluids bathing the tissues and cause there the "reaction" of the body to this germ, for the same reaction occurs no matter where the germ may be growing in the body. This reaction is decidedly inflammatory, the joints swell up because of the exudation from the engorged blood vessels, the delicately sensitive nerve endings in the tissues are pressed upon by the swelling, and this pressure causes the intense pain which is characteristic of this disease, when the invading germ is highly virulent and the patient's body is highly susceptible to the growth of the germ itself. If the organism be not so highly virulent, or the resistance of the individual be comparatively high, the inflammatory reaction in the joints will be correspondingly mild, and the "rheumatism" not so painful or marked. It will be seen therefore why this particular disease may vary from a very slight attack which passes away quickly if the patient's resistance be high and the germs easily be overcome and their toxin neutralized to an "attack" that may last for months and exhaust the patient's strength with pain.

OSTEOPATHY BUILDS UP THE BODY'S OWN RESISTANCE

In such cases of "rheumatism," whether mild or virulent, the germ and its toxin not only attack the joints of the body in general, but also the joints in the spine, causing considerable tissue injury and consequent tensity along the spine and interfering, much or little, as the case may be, with the spinal nerves and their control, indirectly thru their connections with the sympathetic nerves, of those cells of the body that are concerned with the making of the antibodies that neutralize the toxins of the germ and cause the germs to be removed from the tissues. This principle of osteopathy applies in so-called articular rheumatism also, and osteopathy can be depended upon to facilitate and to accelerate the body reactions which ultimately (though more slowly) enable the body to recover from the disease by the use of its own mechanism of resistance. Treating the infected spine of such a patient by the use of osteopathic technique is an absolutely sound procedure, grounded on thoroly scientific theory and practice, and results vindicate the osteopath's contention that the spinal tissue lesion in infectious diseases (when such lesion is actually caused by the infection in the first place) is the block to nature in her attempt to overcome the infection by supplying the remedy which nature itself has planted in the body. Furthermore, osteopathic treatment is the only available treatment in this infection, no serum or vaccine having ever been found which can do the work, altho vast effort has been made in this direction.

"RHEUMATIC" HEART

One of the unpleasant results of so-called articular rheumatism, or rather one of the results of the general infection which is the cause of that disease, is a lesion of the heart that is generally known as "rheumatic heart", altho it is easily seen, in view of what we have already said about rheumatism in general, that the word "rheumatic" here has really no definite meaning whatever. The bacteria (streptococcus pyogenes) being carried into the blood stream, and by it to the joints, also frequently settle on the heart valves, and are likewise carried into the small blood vessels that nourish the muscle wall of the heart, plugging up the vessels, the toxin causing the vessel wall to thicken and harden, thus producing an arteriosclerosis in the organ, and at the same time destroying a certain amount of the muscle tissue of the heart itself. This kind of a heart is the typical "rheumatic heart", and it can, in common with the inflammation of the joints in this disease, be prevented to a high degree by osteopathic treatment in the early stages of the infection. Patients with articular rheumatism, in justice to themselves, should call in an osteopath early in their infection, no matter what their medical doctor may say about it, for the medical doctor professedly can do nothing for such a patient but call daily and look on, prescribing the usual anodynes, usually with danger to the patient's heart, and advising chloroform liniment or other liniments, which are at best the most superficial kind of makeshift. One of the last procedures in these cases is for the doctor to advise the calling in of some masseur, Swedish or other, at a stage of the disease when the slightest touch is condign punishment for the patient, and then, when all things fail, the patient is reluctantly told to try Hot Springs, Mudlavia, or some oher popular cure for rheumatism, and the patient is carried out on a stretcher exhausted in body, mind and pocketbook.

THE EARLIER OSTEOPATHY IS APPLIED, THE BETTER

To how many sufferers is this story familiar? And how much of this expense can be saved will be known only when, with popular enlightenment and education, the victim of streptococcus pyogenes (in the form of "articular rheumatism"), learns to avail himself of the virtue of scientific osteopathic treatment in the earliest stages of the disease.

Long before bacteriologists and pathologists found and identified many of the different germs that cause disease, osteopaths knew that by their own peculiar manipulation and adjustment of the bones and softer tissues of the spine they could stop different infections, reduce temperature, and, in short, work a cure of the disease. Thus the osteopath is not only the sole doctor in cases of the so-called rheumatisms directly caused by anatomical lesions, but is also one of the most important factors in the treatment of rheumatisms, neuritis, neuralgias, lumbagos and sciaticas due to infections wherever they may be.

WHEN DUE TO PUS POCKETS

Aside from articular rheumatism so called, there are many more or less severe pains and inflammations generally labeled rheumatism, caused by pus-forming germs that find lodgment and grow in various parts of the body, often in the mouth of the roots of the teeth, or in the tonsils, or in other parts of the body such as the kidney, for example. The pus-forming bacteria that are the main offenders in this respect are staphylococcus pyogenes aureus and streptococcus pyogenes— the identical germ that causes articular rheumatism—(pyogenes meaning "pus-making", and pus meaning dead white cells of the blood that have lost their lives by ingesting, or taking in, the germs and killing them, in the body's attempt to

get rid of these invading germs in a natural way).
Pockets of these bacteria with their accompany-
ing pus, may continue in some corner of the body
for years, and produce their toxins which in turn
cause the pains of so-called rheumatism, strong
pains if the organism be virulent and the patient
highly susceptible, mild pains if the reverse be
true. In such cases it is of course needful to remove the pus pockets by operation on or even ex-
traction of the teeth, if the germs be growing
there, or by operation on the tonsil if that be the
place of growth, and the removal of the germs will
be followed by spontaneous recovery if all the
centers of germ growth be removed.

PULLING TEETH RUTHLESSLY ANOTHER ERROR

But great care in diagnosis is necessary before
these things be done, and the patient should not be
deprived of teeth or tonsils without a thoroly scientific examination. The removal of the teeth as a
cure for "rheumatic" pains has run riot of late,
and many a man and woman has had good and useful teeth extracted for the cure of some localized
chronic pain, without deriving the slightest benefit
from such a serious operation. In localized "rheumatic" pain it is mainly the anatomical lesion—
the strain, the tensity, the mal-adjustment of tissue and bone, that should be looked for first and
above all things. After this it is well enough to
figure upon pus pockets in the vicinity—pain in
the leg from pelvic infection, and so on. General-
ized pains most frequently are the indicators of
long continued centers of pus-making infection.

But the doctor who would have the teeth extracted from every patient with general or local "rheumatism" of any kind, is a dangerous man to be at large, and too many of that kind of doctors are licensed to practice medicine by unenlightened law.

WHEN RESULTING FROM INTESTINAL PUTREFACTION

Another source of "rheumatic pains" not yet discussed and a most common and important one, is what is known as intestinal auto-intoxication. This consists of the manufacture of poisonous substances by the decomposition of undigested food in the intestine, the "food" consisting of protein, that is meat, eggs, or fish. Such decomposition, or putrefaction, is encompassed by the germs that normally grow in the intestine by the inconceivable billions. One-third of the dried contents of the large intestine consists by weight, of bacteria, but these bacteria are normally harmless. The heavy meat eater acts as a purveyor of food for these germs in the intestine, and large numbers of persons are diet-sick in this way. Reduction of meat in the diet to a reasonable degree will do more to cure rheumatisms from this cause than any other kind of treatment; but this method of dieting has nothing to do with the old-time tradition that red meats are bad for the rheumatic patient. Dieting in that way will not do much to cure or relieve anything.

What used to be called rheumatic neuralgia of the muscles of the abdomen in the vicinity of the stomach has in numerous cases been found to be what is called "flatulent indigestion". For some obscure reason—in some cases maybe a nervous one—the lining of the intestine does not secrete its normal juices, or secretes them in too small a quantity. There is hence a consequent deficiency in power of the secretion of the great digestive organ, the pancreas, owing to the very malfunctioning of the intestine. The result is that the starches do not digest in the intestine, fermentation follows, the intestine is charged with gas, and the pressure causes pain in the region of the stomach, and you have rheumatic neuralgia, or neuralgic rheumatism, for it is all one, so far as the real disorder is concerned. Mineral waters and other laxatives and purgatives fail. Many of such cases are directly traceable to osteopathic lesions in the spine which can be corrected with subsequent relief and disappearance of all symptoms; and when the disorder is due to reflex tensity of the softer tissues of the spine, correction of these accomplish the same result.

GONORRHEAL ARTHRITIS

Another disease that was formerly called rheumatism, and a disease unfortunately by no means rare, is due to an escape into the blood of the germ called gonococcus, which causes by its primary growth in the urinary passages, the venereal disease called gonorrhea. This disease is most frequently acquired by immoral living, and communicated to innocent ones by the guilty. Perhaps some will say that such disease should be discussed only in the consultation room of the physician, and it is this very false "modesty" that has accomplished the physical wreckage and in thousands of cases the death of the unfortunate wife of the libertine husband. Popular knowledge in these things is now being widely cultivated and spread abroad under the name "sexual hygiene", and vast suffering and social error might have been saved in the past had every young woman, and the parents of every young woman possessed such information on these subjects as would have safe-guarded the innocent victim of an unwise marriage.

And yet even with the most careful scrutiny it is almost impossible to guard the innocent or enable the uninfected to guard against deception when dealing with an unconscionable and ignorant man. Such men themselves are the main victims of this disease, and it is in many ways a pity that disastrous consequences do not as a rule follow the usual infection. Then perhaps this social evil would stop or prevent itself. This germ does not only itself produce pus centers in the body, but it also paves the way for the entrance into the body of other pus-making organisms which work the final disaster, disabling or causing the death of the infected person by a mixed infection. But when this germ enters the blood and settles out for its further growth in the joints of the body it produces what has in recent times been called gonorrheal arthritis, or an inflammation of the joints similar in some ways to articular rheumatism, and

111

in others different from that disease. Frequently in such cases the germs, like streptococcus pyogenes, settle on the heart, causing the heart lesion called endocarditis, altho endocarditis can be, and usually is, caused in other and less disastrous ways. This kind of rheumatism has been treated by vaccines but not with the success which would be desirable, and osteopathy has been found practical and beneficient in these cases, as it has been found in rheumatisms of other kinds.

RHEUMATOID ARTHRITIS

Another species of rheumatism, common in persons who have passed middle-age, is the so-called "rheumatoid arthritis", an inflammation of the joints, which often produces considerable deformity, and even disablement, in many cases causing the patient to become more or less crippled and unable to move about or use the hands with freedom. In all chronic cases of this kind there is absolutely no treatment which yields as good results as osteopathy. Persons whose joints were practically clear out of use, have been relieved in some measure by manipulations which loosen up to a considerable degree the old stiffness, and have been restored, in a measure, to the use of their limbs. When osteopathic treatment can produce such gratifying results in old chronic cases, it is most rational to believe that this infection could be handled in an entirely satisfactory way if taken early in its course.

The osteopathic physician will be careful to consider and look for some primary source of the infection in the tonsils, the teeth or elsewhere, for when the symptoms in the joints begin to appear, it is clear there is some source of infection that has been at work for some time, unperceived by the patient. In such cases it is well to have x-ray shadowgraphs made of the teeth, or other parts, to locate the focus, or foci, of infection, which can be removed by surgery—dental or other—and to let this treatment be intelligently followed up by osteopathic therapy, which will help the body to take care of the germs and their toxins that have escaped and are doing the general tissue destruction at places far removed from the original portals of the invasion.

OSTEOPATHY AVAILABLE IN PAINS OF MECHANICAL AND GERM ORIGIN BOTH

In conclusion one may say the "rheumatic pains", when directly traceable to some comparatively prominent or comparatively obscure tissue disturbance, either in the spine or elsewhere, are reasonably certain to be cured by osteopathic adjustment of the lesions. A large percentage of "rheumatism" is directly caused by these anatomical displacements, tensions, or mal-adjustments, and for all of these osteopathy is the only and at the same time the perfect remedy. In other forms of so-called rheumatism, when the pains are due to the presence of germs in the body, osteopathy may still be relied upon as one of the most important factors in the relief and cure of these infections, especially when the germs or their poisons have rendered the tissues of the

spine tense or hard. And osteopathic treatment
in general may be depended upon as one of the
most salutary measures in maintaining a state of
body well calculated to be resistent to the several
germs that cause the swellings and pains formerly
called rheumatism, as also to other germs and to
germ diseases in general.

CHAPTER VII

HOW THE HUMAN BODY IS OPERATED

In this number I wish to tell my readers the broad reasons why the osteopathic physician has such remarkable control over the human body in all its parts and organs. You often hear this question asked in a sort of surprise that this should be so. You will often hear intelligently curious persons wonder why it is that osteopathy has made such a splendid success as a healing art. A system of therapy that has given to the world so fine a body of practitioners; that year after year is drawing larger and larger numbers of splendid men and women into the ranks of osteopathic practitioners; a system and a science that in a few years have built up so many colleges and is daily growing with a silent and steady power that is its own best recommendation has, of course, beneath it a solid foundation of scientific fact and truth.

To understand this broad foundation I will ask my readers to consider for a while some intensely interesting facts of Nature, out of which the art and science of osteopathy have grown, and upon which this system rests as upon an everlasting foundation. For you must understand that osteopathy did not fall out of the sky like a meteor, but

115

came about in the natural evolution of things just like the wireless telegraph and the electric light. The osteopathic system of therapy became possible from the moment the true structure of the nervous system was discovered, and as that discovery is most intimately associated with a broader and more fundamental discovery, I will ask my reader to follow me for a while in the relation of one of the most amazing stories that has ever been told and in the description of one of the most startling facts that has been brought to the attention of men.

OUR BODIES BUILT FROM CELLS LIKE A HOUSE OF BRICKS

It is now a little more than seventy years since the discovery was made that the bodies of animals, including man, consist of countless billions of microscopic animals called "cells". This epoch-making revelation startled the world when it was announced in 1839 by its discoverer, Theodor Schwann, a young German anatomist and physiologist, who at that time was assistant in the laboratory of Johannes Mueller, professor of anatomy and physiology at the University of Berlin. Previous to Schwann's discovery it had been known that plants were built up of microscopic cells, but nobody had ever suspected that the human body was constructed on the same amazing plan. To understand, in a general way of course, how the human body is constructed, peel an orange, carefully pull it apart into its constituent segments, with your fingers, take one of the smal-

116

lest of these segments and gently break it across as to expose the "meat" of the orange, and then carefully examine the broken surface. The structure of the orange appears as a granular texture. By gently working at this texture you can separate the individual granules so as to remove a few of them from their countless neighbors. The granules, as you can readily see with the unaided eye, are in reality spindle-shaped or roundish bodies, like tiny bladders. Each one of these little bodies is a "cell", and the structure they form—all packed in together tightly and snugly—is a "tissue". The orange cell is one of the few forms of cell visible to the naked eye. It is a little bladder, the wall of which consists of plant fibre, and within the bladder is the sap—the protoplasm of the cell—that potent stuff of which all living matter is composed.

I have said that up to Schwann's discovery it was known that plants, or vegetable bodies, were built up of cells, but it was not suspected that all animal tissues were of the same structure. Plant cells and animal cells have an infinite variety of shapes and sizes, are put together in several different ways, and are almost all individually invisible to the unaided eye. It is this difference in the shape, size and the way the cells are packed together, that form the main differences in the appearance of the different animal tissues—apart from the color and odor of the tissues. The muscles consist of billions of elongated cells, as if the cells of the orange were drawn out to invisibility and packed longitudinally together. When a great muscle, like the biceps, for example, contracts, the contraction is due to the fact that all the invisible muscle cells—called fibres—contract simultaneously together. But in order to see these individual fibres you must take some dead muscle—let us say a tiny bit of beefsteak—soak it in potash solution, in order to dissolve the thready, fibrous "connective tissue" that binds the fibres together, spread the bit of muscle out, and look at it under a microscope, and then you will see the individual fibres—the cells—as plainly, and even much more plainly, than you can see the individual cells in the tissue of an orange.

In the human body the cells of some tissues, like the skin and hair, lie in layers, cells of the topmost layers being flattened into scales; the cells of others are long drawn out as in muscles, the cells of others, such as the liver, the stomach and many other glands, are arranged so as to form tiny tubes, invisible to the unaided eye; and the cells of other organs or parts, like the spleen, are crowded together somewhat after the fashion of the orange. Even the bones consist of living cells, together with substances manufactured by the cells.

It is believed—and it is known for many of the cells—that all the cells of the body are short-lived; that some of them are continually dissolving and are carried away by the blood, but that they leave their descendants behind, just like a community of men: so that while the individual cells may pass away, the community of cells—the organ, or the tissue—continues to live. This is perhaps generally true—with one great exception. That exception is the nerve cell. The nerve cells do not die, and they do not reproduce themselves. The nerve cells of a man in his old age are identical with the nerve cells of infancy. From the time that nerve cells make their first appearance in the growing organism long before birth and on until death, they retain their individuality. They do not reproduce themselves and dissolve, as the other cells do.

In short, nerve cells are in many ways a remarkable exception to the common laws of cell life; and nervous tissues—as we shall presently see—occupies a singular and wonderful position among tissues in general, and is exempt in many ways from the dangers and diseases that threaten all the other tissues of the body. The nerve cells are the rulers of all the other cells of the body—the masters; they bid all the other cells—they force the other cells to do their particular work. They force the muscles to contract; they regulate the flow of the blood in the arteries and veins; they stir up the gland cells—such as those of stomach and liver—to secrete the products of these organs; they control the nourishment of all the various parts of the body; and they alone protect the body from a thousand dangers which, without the ceaseless watching and sleepless vigilance of the nerve cells (for these cells work during sleeping and waking) would flow in upon the body and de-

119

stroy its life. The body may be likened to an ocean steamer of which the nerve cell is the owner, captain, navigator, pilot and eternal look-out man all in one. All the other cells of the body are the obedient crew and ship at one and the same time. I will return to this subject a little later.

The same nerve cells with which a man is born last him throughout his life. This is not true of the other cells of the body. And this fact has an important bearing on the treatment of disease, and especially upon the osteopathic method of treating disease. Other cells of the body may be injured or even destroyed, and they are replaced by the generation of new cells of their kind. But if the nerve cells are permanently injured or destroyed by the long use of drugs or other destructive agents, they can never be replaced by new nerve cells and must remain permanently injured as long as the individual lives. Thus, too, it is readily seen that, as the nerve cells rule the body in all its functions, the osteopath, who controls the nerve cells through their great clearing house, the spinal cord, and indirectly, the brain, has his finger, so to speak, on the switch-board of all these various functions which are directly under control of the nerves themselves.

SCHWANN'S CELL DISCOVERY WAS A FORE-RUNNER OF OSTEOPATHY

Now while it is true that all animals and plants are built up of cells, we find in Nature single cells that live alone—the unicellular, or one-celled animals and plants. Countless billions of these single cells—each an animal or plant in itself—can be found in the water of ponds and pools. Bacteria—the so-called "germs", a few of which produce disease when they lodge in the body and multiply there—are exceedingly minute single cells: as if an orange cell were to be reduced to, say 1-50,000 or 1-25,000 of an inch, and were to multiply itself all alone without association with its fellow cells. So, too, we find innumerable single animal cells that live in water, or damp places, all of which are visible only in the microscope. When you see under the microscope the wonderful, the almost intelligent conduct and maneuvering of one of these exceedingly small animal cells, you are deeply impressed with the littleness and magnitude of Nature.

Remember, now, that these little single-celled animals were well known before Schwann made his discovery that the human body was only a great co-ordinated mass of tiny individual animals, packed together, put together, strung and woven together in inconceivable complexity and unthinkable numbers, and you may have some idea of how startled the world was when men were first informed of that fact. It was really an almost incredible thing; and it is by no means a comfortable

A single nerve cell from the spinal cord, (A) the long-drawn-out fibre which, when bound together with millions of its fellows, makes a nerve trunk, or nerve, as we see it in the body. (B) the body of the cell with its nucleus, and the branching network of connecting fibres.

thing; and to be told that one's brain consists of billions of individual microscopic animals; all working together like a perfect trained army. Yet, such is the fact; and when Schwann announced that fact in 1839 he was unconsciously laying the foundations of the modern science and art of osteopathy.

SOME OF THE STRUCTURES AND PROPERTIES OF NERVE CELLS

If you take a little piece of the spinal cord, or spinal marrow, of an ox, or any other animal (a fish does excellently) and let it soak over night in weak alcohol or chloral hydrate, and then mash a tiny bit of it between two pieces of thin glass and look at it in a microscope, you will see a sight that should not only startle and amaze you, but should instruct you as well. You will see nerve cells, pretty much as they exist in your own spinal cord—pretty much as they exist in the living brain and spinal cord of a man. Wonderful things they are. There is an irregularly-shaped central body of a dull grayish color, like ground glass, from which stretch forth in many directions, long sinuous arms, like the "feelers" of a cuttlefish. In the middle of the central body is a round body that looks like an eye. It is not an eye. It is the vital organ of the nerve cell, and if some carmine has been mixed with the bit of spinal cord this round eye-like body in the center of the nerve cell will be stained red. This is the nucleus of the cell (and all cells of every kind have a nucleus). The nucleus is the vital part of the cell

122

and upon its life the life of the whole cell depends. All the "feelers" thrown out by the nerve cell are richly branched, like the limbs of a tree, breaking up into minute twigs; all with one exception. This exceptional "feeler" (and these processes from the nerve cell are literally and truly "feelers") has few branches and, unlike the other "feelers" (technically called dendrites from the Greek word for tree), it does not terminate near the cell body but continues on for enormous distances. This long feeler is called the "fibre" and in company with thousands of other fibres from other nerve cells in the spinal cord, it runs out of the tube formed by the vertebrae of the backbone, and forms its tiny part of what is called a nerve. The nerve cells are in the spinal cord, and the fibres leave the cord (or the brain, for the brain is built up in the same way of cells) and in the great cables of fibres called nerves the fibres run to all parts of the body. The fibres constitute the white matter of nervous tissue, so called because of a fatty substance which surrounds and insulates the fibres, and is called the "white substance of Schwann", Schwann having discovered it. This white sheath is also called by other names, but the white color of nerve is due to the white fatty sheath that surrounds each individual fibre.

A nerve fibre bound up with thousands of others in a nerve will run from the cell in the cord without a break clear to the finger or toe tip, where it ends in the skin. If you prick the skin of the finger the impulse is carried up the fibre to the cell in the cord, and there the cell passes the impulse to another nerve cell, and so on up to the gray matter (the cells) of the brain, where the impulse is "felt" as sensation.

To convey some practical notion of the real size of the nerve cell together with the length of some of the longest of the fibres, we may compare it with a much larger object. There are nerve cells in the spinal cord about 1-100th of an inch in diameter or less with minute fibres coming from them, so small as to be visible only in the microscope Many thousands of these fibres are gathered together and bound tightly with connective tissue so as to form the cable-like nerve trunks which pass out of the tube-like cavity of the backbone. These cables of nerve fibres and their cable-like branches—the nerves—vary in thickness from the diameter of a lead pencil down to a much smaller size, and after they leave the backbone they break up into smaller branches which supply the muscles and skin of the upper and lower parts of the body, giving off smaller and smaller bundles of fibres as they recede from the spine, until finally the nerve is broken up into

A Motor Nerve Cell from the Spinal Cord. We get our power of motion through cells like this. Note its net-work of branches at its base for establishing communication with other Nerve Cells.

124

branches no longer visible except in the microscope. These invisible bundles of fibres ultimately branch until they separate into the still smaller individual fibres which connect with almost all the cells of the tissues and stimulate them into action. It is the little nerve fibres that cause the muscle cell to contract, the gland cell to secrete, and so on.

Certain nerve cells in the spinal cord send their minute fibres all the way without a break to the foot. Let us take one of these, say one whose fibre goes to the tip of the great toe, supplying it with nerves of sensation. Let us imagine that this nerve cell in the cord were the size of an ordinary water-bucket. Its fibre then would be proportionately thicker and longer. It would be about as thick as a broomstick and would be about two miles long! A man who would be big enough to have nerve cells and nerve fibres of that size would measure about two miles from the end of his backbone to the soles of his feet; and if the rest of his body were in proportion he would be in all nearly four miles high! Such a man could almost breathe ordinary men in and out of his nostrils without inconvenience. Of these nerve cells each with its own fibre, it is estimated that there are in the brain and spinal cord about two thousand millions.

The nerve cells and their intercommunications in the human organism make up a system which probably possesses more apparatus and contains more mysteries a hundred-fold than all the electric systems of our country.

The spinal nerves furnish the muscles and skin with the fibres that give motion and sensation to these organs. In the skin the fibres break up into still smaller fibrils, and end in strange looking bulbs, which furnish the skin with organs of touch. Some of these nerve endings, as they are called, are sensitive to cold only; others to heat only; others to touch only; and you can prove this by lightly touching the skin here and there with a cold pencil point or blunt pointed metallic rod, and noting the "cold spots" and so on. The skin is crowded so thickly with these nerve endings that even if all the other tissues of a man were wiped out—if he had nothing but his nervous system left—you could still easily recognize his face from the nerve endings alone. Now as each sensitive ending of a fibre has a corresponding fibre which runs to some muscle fibre, the sensory and motor apparatuses of the body work in perfect harmony. If the skin of the toe be pricked the impulse travels to the cord along a fibre of sensation and is there transferred to motor cells which send impulses to the muscles that move the leg, and the foot is instantly withdrawn. This is called reflex action and when the physician taps below the knee of his patient to "test his reflex" he is using this mechanism. If we could dissolve away all the tissues of the body except the nervous system, there would be left a phantom of a man whom we could easily recognize and identify from the nerve endings in the skin. So that we thus

126

see that the nervous system is ever on the watch at the farthest outposts for danger to the body.

Through these millions of microscopic sense organs in the skin, that great mass of nerve cells and fibres called the brain, is instantaneously warned of all danger. The nerve fibres of the ear, of the nose, of the tongue and of the skin generally, serve the double purpose of assisting the body to get its food, to enjoy all pleasurable things whatsoever, to stimulate the body to move about from place to place, or to move the muscles without change of location. But these wonderful sense organs do more. They bring instant warning of danger. They tell us when to fly from danger, when to avoid the sources of danger in disagreeable odors, sights, sounds, or tastes, when to seek refuge from the cold or heat, and in every movement of the body guide it and direct it aright. The nerve endings in the skin sound the alarm from dangers without, and the nerve endings in the internal organs and

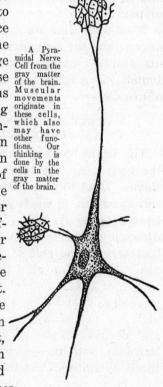

A Pyramidal Nerve Cell from the gray matter of the brain. Muscular movements originate in these cells, which also may have other functions. Our thinking is done by the cells in the gray matter of the brain.

127

parts warn us of danger from within by report-
ing to the brain every abnormal, or nearly every
abnormal, condition that invades us. Thus we
see that the nervous system with its great shadowy, veil-like mantle of nerve endings, acts like a
protecting vapor to the body, and, by means of
the voluntary muscles, which are the mere slaves
of the brain and the spinal cord, commands the
body to move towards and do things that give
pleasure and comfort, and to move away from
and to avoid doing things that bring discomfort
or pain.

It is upon this master system of tissue, the
nerves, and the demonstration of their control by
his skillful manipulations, that the osteopath
founds his science for the prevention and cure
of disease.

ALL OTHER STRUCTURES VASSALS OF THE BRAIN AND NERVES

The brain and the nerves are the masters of
the body. All the other organs and parts are
slaves. And to give pleasure and comfort to itself the brain compels all the other organs and
tissues to do its will. This will is, as a rule,
directed so that when the brain and nerves are
best served, the rest of the body is best served
also. The best good of the brain and the nerves,
therefore, is as a general rule, the best good of the
slave organs and tissues too. But this, unfortunately, is not always the case. When the will
and desires of the nervous system are not in
harmony with the general welfare of the body,
the body suffers. As the nerve tissue is the ab-

128

solute master, the muscles must obey it, even when its mandates are destructive or insane. Therefore the nervous system, to gratify its own wants, will often destroy the useful slaves that minister to its needs. Like the soldiers in the fatal charge at Balaclava, the muscles and the other tissues obey without question.

> Theirs not to make reply,
> Theirs not to reason why,
> Theirs—but to do and die.

So the nervous system, to gratify its capricious and destructive desires, often compels the muscles to feed the body with poisonous drugs and stimulants and to do other things that not only destroy the slaves, but in the end the master, also, that is served and nourished by the slaves. The stomach, the liver, the kidneys, the pancreas, the intestines, the lungs and the other glands, and above all the voluntary muscles, are often ruined and wrecked by the intemperate or abnormal desires of the nervous system. The brain, seated upon an imperial throne, whose mandates are instantly and absolutely obeyed, is often an insane Nero dealing death and ruin around him and ending as only such insane tyrants can end, in death and destruction for himself.

There is, however, another view of the nervous system in which the blame cannot be laid upon the nervous system itself. The nervous system, in spite of all its superb machinery of self-protection and self-gratification, can be injured in many ways, and *not* receive warning to avoid the danger.

The nervous system, for example, may be compelled to work overtime. It, too, may be a slave in its turn; and in very fact the nervous system, with the remainder of the body, is itself a slave to a power higher than itself. This power may be single or two-fold. It may consist of defects or faults in the heritage of the nervous system itself. Or it may consist in the defects and faults that have been inherited by the other organs and tissues from parents. These would be defects of inheritance. The defects may be due again to the circumstances in which the individual human being, or other organism, is compelled to live. These would be defects of environment. But a normal nervous system, surrounded by defective organs is really a nervous system in an unhealthy environment. So we see that, given a naturally sound nervous system, such a nervous system may suffer

A Sympathetic Nerve Cell such as is found in man's Solar Plexus. Cells like this never sleep—they automatically run and regulate all of life's processes, night and day from birth to death.

from being lodged first in a body the organs of which are unhealthy because of unhealthy parents, or because of disease due to malformations, mal-alignments or mal-adjustments in the structure of the tissues that surround the nervous system, or by poisons in the body, which, although they may not affect the nervous system itself, do disable the slave tissues and make them incapable of obeying the orders of the nerves, even when the orders are given with clear enunciation and the best intent for the common good. Such a nervous system would be disabled, more or less, by the defects of its organic environment; by the defects in the tissues, the organs, and the fluids of the body in which the healthy normal nervous system is lodged.

Secondly, the nervous system may be stopped or disabled by the poisons which accumulate in the blood and other fluids of the body, and in the tissues, because of overwork or of unhealthy surroundings in which the human being is compelled to live—in spite of the warnings which the nerve endings in the skin and eyes, ears and nose, and in all the other parts of the body, convey to the brain. In this case the nervous system is once more a slave to its environment. In either case—whether from poisons present in the body through inheritance of defective organs from parents; or from disease; or from overwork, or other faults in the organic environment ("lesions"), the nervous system is itself a slave, and its commands to its own slaves—the other tissues—are not obeyed.

Now, while we hear a great deal about nervous diseases, the truth is that true diseases of the nervous system are comparatively rare. What I mean is that there are innumerable diseases—let us call it "bad health" using contradictory terms of the layman, which have generally a sound sense bottom, by the way—there are many diseases, or much "bad health" that manifest themselves in the nervous system without being nervous diseases at all. The nervous system in such cases is perfectly sound and well, but it seems to be sick and shattered because it is surrounded by poisons in the fluids of the body and by organs which, because of the poisons, are disabled as regards obeying the commands of the nervous system when they are uttered. In these cases—which form perhaps 90 per cent of all diseases, or "bad health"—the apparent nervous disorder is not a true nervous disorder, but only the frantic incessant activity of the brain and nerves to force the other organs to do their duty when, alas, these other organs are deaf to the command—disabled by defects of structure or by poisons which nullify the nerve message.

It is truly wonderful how perfectly resistant to disease or disorder of any kind the nervous system is! Ages of development and necessity have successively selected for survival only the most strongly resistant nervous systems, so that very few weak nervous systems remain. All our predecessors—or nearly all—that had weak nervous systems were wiped out before they could get children. Therefore, only the strongest—the most immune—nervous systems survive. This is the "survival of the fittest" and the great law of natural selection is seen best exemplified in the security, the strength, the immunity, the imperial power and sanctity of brain and nerve in all the bewildering and manifold forms of life. When a man, or other animal, is starved to death, the nervous system is the very last to suffer from loss of weight. All the tissues, all the organs, give up their substance first to the brain and nerves, and next to the muscles. This, you see, is good policy on the part of Nature, for the reason that if the nerves suffered and lost power, they could not stimulate the muscles to move about, secure food, and bring it to the mouth. In starvation, the body weight is reduced two-thirds before the nervous system loses a grain's weight of substance. Very few germs attack nerve tissue. The nerves are attacked by the poison of the tetanus germ, and by the germ of hydrophobia. But the number of germs and germ poisons which attack nerve tissue is comparatively small. So-called "disorders of the nerves" are really not nerve disorders at all, but the efforts of the nervous system—the frantic commands and over-activity of the nerves—to restore order to the disordered body in which they find themselves.

A frog sympathetic nerve cell.

Unfortunately the rule of the old school medicine has been to treat the nerves in these cases by the administration of drug "tonics" and other medicines. This practice is now happily being abandoned by scientifically educated and intelligent doctors of the old school, who have come to know that the only nerve tonics which can help the nerves are good food and good blood. But the truth is that "nervous symptoms" are in reality a proof not of the sickness of the nerves, but of their health, in most cases! The nervous system is sound in all cases save the few in which the nerve tissue itself is at fault. The osteopath here is on the right track and always has been. And to the view of the osteopath the other doctors are coming round, only they have neither the knowledge nor the skill of the osteopath to get at the root of the business by handling the nervous system in a way that will give to it the extra power it needs to force the organs into normal response.

The cure for all toxins in the body lies in the fluids and tissues of the body itself!

BODY'S CHEMICAL ACTION UNDER CONTROL OF THE NERVES

What, let us ask, is a "healthy" man? The answer is, a healthy man is an animal the cells of whose organs and tissues have the power of full and instantaneous response to the commands of the nervous system, when these commands are directed for the good and the comfort, not only of the brain and nerves themselves, but for the ease and comfort of the other tissues also. Recall, now, that the nervous system consists of microscopic cells with long tiny microscopic fibres, that often at long distances from the nerve cells themselves, connect up with all the principal other cells of the body. When you are told that the minute invisible fibres of the nerve cells in the brain and cord are connected with other nerve cells in the body cavity called the sympathetic (or involuntary) nerves, and that these involuntary cells have fibres that ramify infinitely to each individual cell of all the organs—of the digestive, the genito-urinary, the respiratory systems—and to each individual cell of the heart and the blood vessels (for the heart and the blood vessels, too, are built up of cells) ; and that every cell of every other important organ, such as the mysterious "ductless glands" like the thyroid, the mysterious ovaries and testicles with their unknown secretions that affect the health and well being of the entire body, the mysterious suprarenal glands, and other organs of that peculiar kind—when you are told all this, you will come to a slight realization of the tremendous sway which the nervous system has over the infinitely intricate chemical life of the body. The cells of the organs cannot act unless bidden by the nerve fibres. If the cells are poisoned by toxins, whether from the body cells themselves or from invading germs, the mandates that pour along the nerve fibres from the nerve cells, bidding the organ cells to secrete, or bidding other cells do other things, are blocked; and finding their mandates blocked, the nerve cells over-exert themselves in extraordinary commands to the cells of the other organs to do what the other organs cannot do because of the poisons that bathe them all around.

Now how does the osteopath answer the question which the body of his patient puts to him?

If the blocking of the commands of the nerve cells be due to some impingement on the nerves by reason of a faulty articulation, or an over-tension or congestion of the ligaments and muscles, or other maladjustment of the spine, or elsewhere, he corrects the maladjustment, removes the block, and the nerve, which was healthy enough all the while, can now convey its message to the organ cell—which was also healthy all the while; and the "disorder" is cured.

If on the other hand the blocking be due, not to any such maladjustment—lesion it is called by the osteopath— but is due to some defect in the organ cells themselves by reason of inheritance; or is due to defects in the cells by reason of poisons in the fluids which bathe them, the osteopath reinforces the power of the nerves by vastly increasing the strength of the commands sent along the fibres to the organ cells. To the impulses naturally flowing down the tiny nerve fibres from the nerve cells in the spinal cord and the brain, his fingers, skilfully touching the great nerve trunks, add a thousand-

The "Skeleton" of the nervous sytem as it would look if its visible structure were disassociated from all the rest of the body.

136

fold power so that to the master nerve cells' own power of command is brought this tremendous aid from the outside environment—an aid and ally which can come to the nerve by no other means except that which the osteopathic physician uses, and which is one of the main foundation stones of the science and art of osteopathy itself. That is what I meant a while ago when I said that when Theodor Schwann discovered that the nervous system consisted of individual cells with long drawn out fibres, he made it possible for A. T. Still, M. D., in our time to lay the foundations of the modern science of osteopathy; and by this time, I believe, the reader will have been sufficiently enlightened to see the truth of that assertion.

Sectional drawing illustrating how the nerves from the Cerebro-Spinal and Sympathetic systems ramify to all the organs. This reveals the nerve-routes through which osteopathic fingers "telegraph" vital messages from the posterior (sensory) nerves, through the spinal cord and brain, to the internal organs.

The nerves, then, control the chemism of the body and its organs and this chemism or chemical reaction, being controlled by the nerves, is hence also under the control of the osteopath. Thus the osteopath plays upon the natural chemism of the body, avoiding the use of nerve-destroying drugs. In former times the old drug therapy sought mainly to find drugs which by acting on the various nerve centers to increase or diminish their activity, would by that route control the body's functions. But it was forgotten that this control was often secured at the expense of destroying the natural automatic regulation of the body by the nervous system. Health was not restored. The nerves were merely unduly excited or depressed and the artificial effects of this treatment were mistaken for actual cures.

So, too, it can readily be seen that this direct connection with all the organs of the body by the nervous system is the very thing which makes it possible for the vital processes of one person to pass under the direction, and to a considerable extent the control of, the finger of another applied externally to the body. The trained hands of the osteopathic physician, applied to the spinal switchboard of the patient, bring health to bodily functions by normalizing all tissues and especially the nerve centers and the organs they command.

CHAPTER VIII

"THE BLOOD IS THE LIFE" AND HOW OSTEOPATHY KEEPS IT PURE

Ever since the far-off day when men first acquired the habit of leaving behind them written records of their thoughts and doings, the blood has been an object of prime interest and attention. Even long before that time, blood must have been a principal theme of thought and discussion; for not only men but the carnivorous lower animals themselves are always conscious, or sub-conscious, of blood and its uses and importance, not alone as associated with the slaughter of animals used for food, but also as the hot fluid which pulses in the arteries and flows in the veins, the brilliant red color of which is so glaringly and strikingly vivid when, upon the slightest puncture of the skin, it leaps into view.

The mere sight of blood has often a peculiar psychic effect upon certain sensitive persons. I once knew a certain anatomist of wide reputation, who grew dizzy whenever he saw blood. He had seen dissected thousands of dead men without a qualm, but to see a tiny trickling from the marvelous red river of life tended to make him swoon. In all other ways he was a strong man. No other sight could shock him. But the sight of blood made him sick.

There is a reason for all this human interest in blood, and that reason is the ancient inherited instinct that tells us, with an emphasis which no mere experience can give, that the Prophet was right when he said that "the blood is the life". Men knew that to bleed meant to die, and in fact all those animals whose blood did not have the property of quickly clotting were eliminated before they could produce offspring, so that only those animals whose blood clotted survived. Were it not for its property of clotting at the wound, thus closing the wound and stopping the flow, the blood would keep on flowing from a small wound until the animal, or the man, were dead.

But ancient as is the importance of blood in the thoughts of men, the blood is regarded with infinitely more interest today than it ever was; and if the ancient prophet could say with truth that the blood was the life, the scientist of today can assert with equal force that it is more than life. We can say with positive conviction that the blood is also the forestaller of death; that the blood is the great stream along which float the countless protecting hosts of the body that ward off the agents of destruction that threaten us from without, and build up the breaches that have been made within. The blood not only carries nourishment to every minute chink and cell of the body, and carries away, as in a great sewer system, the waste matters of the tissue—such as carbon dioxide, urea, water and other ashes and debris of the slow combustion called metabolism constantly going on in the tissues—but it likewise bears in its swift-flowing stream we know not how many substances that protect the body from harm—substances that have been inherited from the most remote ancestors, or that have been newly introduced into the blood by disease. For a disease often acts as its own cure and prevention for the future—immunity this is called.

ALL THE FACTS OF MODERN RESEARCH CONFIRM OSTEOPATHY

In previous months I have told you about the high importance which the osteopathic physician attaches to the nerves, with their millions of invisible fibers that ramify to almost all of the countless billion of cells of which the body is made up. But the osteopathic physician also realizes the importance of the blood as the great agent through which, with the cells as the intermediaries between the blood and the nerves, the nerves can react indirectly on all the tissues and even on the nerve-cells and nerve-fibers themselves.

In this review I shall try to tell you a few of the facts upon which osteopathy founds its theory and practice in the treatment of disease of every kind; for modern osteopaths have merely seized upon and taken for themselves the great body of facts which science—working quite without regard to the cure of disease—has discovered for itself during the past century.

To give you an example of how long and patiently investigators will labor with a problem, let us consider the question of the clotting of the blood. The first modern investigators of the causes of the clotting of the blood were John Hunter (1728-1793) and William Hewson (1767), who asked themselves the question, "Why does the blood clot?" and who independently undertook a most interesting (and now historical) series of experiments with the answer to the question in view. Hunter and Hewson merely broke the ice of the problem, however, and it is only within the past decade that a satisfactory answer has been provided. Hunter was struck with the fact that the blood clotted when it was shed. Why did it not clot in the vessels? One hundred reasons (at a guess) were assumed, and had to be rejected, one after another, when experiment proved them false. And it is only after one hundred and fifty years that the problem has been worked out with a measurable degree of satisfaction. But the problem is not solved yet! For each new discovery has opened up new problems that await new answers; and it has been found that to understand the clotting of the blood in any degree of thoroughness it will be necessary to understand the very nature of matter itself!

For nearly 140 years physiologists had been investigating the chemical nature of the blood in all sorts of ingenious experiments; and, while their progress had been good in its way, it was infinitely slow when compared with the rapid work and the truly remarkable discoveries that have been made within the past 20 or 25 years in the various laboratories of the world—in Europe principally, of course.

The modern era of our knowledge of the blood in disease dates in reality less than 20 years ago, in one respect, and less than 30 years ago in another. I will recur to this difference a little later, but first you must understand what the blood is, in so far as it is possible to understand it at all.

Many years ago Macallum, the physiologist of the University of Toronto, analyzed the blood of animals (including man) in comparison with sea water, and found that the blood was very similar in many of its constitutents to the water of the sea.

The blood of animals (including man) consists of water in which are dissolved the chlorides, phosphates, carbonates and sulphates of sodium, calcium, potassium and magnesium in about the percentage in which these saline substances are found in sea water. Sea water contains many other salts dissolved in it, but this may be neglected for the present. Also dissolved in the water of the blood are found substances being carried to the tissues and waste matters on their way towards excretion. Macallum suggested the interesting theory that the liquid part of the blood of animals had been originally inherited from bloodless ancestors — inhabitants of the sea — with water circulation like the sponge and other similar animals, whose circulatory system consisted of an intricate labyrinth of canals (vessels) with outer openings into which poured the water of the sea, to pour out again back into the sea from other openings, or pores. If we imagine that the openings through which the water flowed in and out were to close up; that the vessels, or channels, or canals, through generations of slow change, were to develop a heart; that the sea water were retained within the vessels, and was gradually supplied from the animal's tissues with specially developed cells, which floated in it as their natural habitat; and that the digested food were absorbed into the water in the vessels through the walls of the vessels from the stomach — why, then, we would have animal blood just as it is today, with its sodium chloride and some other mineral salts (in the same proportion as these salts exist in sea water), with its red and white corpuscles—that is, the floating cells, and all the rest of it.

Now this idea of Macallum's gives you a very fair rough notion of what blood really is. It is water with a few mineral salts (such as sodium chloride and others) dissolved in it; with digested (that is, dissolved) food in it; with the waste substances of the body dissolved in it (as the waste substances of the sponge's body are dissolved in the water that pours out of its canals into the sea) ; and with many other substances dissolved in it, of which I am about to tell you now.

It is in these other substances, as well as in the food and waste matters in the blood, that the osteopath is interested, for he, like his forerunner, the physician of the old school, realizes that health depends upon the perfect, or nearly perfect, equilibrium that maintains between the poisons that may enter the blood from without, through the activities of germs that lodge in the body (or the poisons that may be made by the body itself), and the neutralization of these substances by anti-poisons in the blood. This again is what is called immunity.

FOUNDER OF OSTEOPATHY

Four great names are associated with the rapid development of the modern era of our knowledge of the blood. These are Ehrlich, Pfeiffer, Bordet and Metchnikoff. Ehrlich is the world-renowned pathologist of the royal serum institute at Frankfort. Pfeiffer is another noted German investigator, who has done much to advance the science of the blood. Bordet is one of the tireless workers of the Pasteur Institute at Paris, and Metchnikoff, Russian by birth, is perhaps the greatest of all the ingenious experimenters in that famous institution.

If the osteopathic physician had nothing but the facts which these four men alone have added to human knowledge, he would have sufficient to explain, on scientific grounds, the amazing chemical mechanism of the blood and the tissues that underlie all the results which osteopathy gets—often to the amazement of the patient and the old school practitioner—in the treatment of diseases which the osteopath handles by causing blood to flow in unusual quantities to the parts of the body involved, or with unusual rapidity to all parts when toxic substances are generally distributed or by using the nerves to stimulate the cells of the body in their efforts to manufacture the anti-poisons which neutralize the poisons absorbed.

But let us begin with Pfeiffer.

It had been known that normal blood serum (that is, the clear, straw-colored fluid that separates naturally from clotted blood) would kill certain germs, such as typhoid or cholera bacilli. These bacilli are exceedingly minute rod-like bodies that are clearly visible only in the highest powers of the microscope, and measure in length about 1/12,500 of an inch. When the blood of a guinea pig, for example, is shed, and some of the clear serum that separates out from the clot is mixed with some living typhoid or cholera germs stirred up in salt solution, the living, motile germs are suddenly stricken motionless and soon are partly dissolved, or eaten away, as a lump of sugar is attacked and eaten away (dissolved) by water.

This fact had been discovered in 1888 by a young American, Nuttall, who was working in a German laboratory. One year later a German bacteriologist, Bucher, showed that if such a serum be heated to a little beyond half way to boiling (55 deg. Centigrade) it would no longer destroy the living germs.

Moved by these facts Pfeiffer decided to make an experiment with a living animal, in order to see how far the animal could be made to destroy, in its proper living body, the living virulent germs of cholera or typhoid. Now it was known that an untreated normal guinea pig had the power of killing and dissolving a small number of typhoid or cholera germs when the germs were injected into the cavity between the inner wall of the abdomen and the outer wall of the intestine. This cavity is called the peritoneal cavity. Pfeiffer injected into this cavity of a guinea pig increasing doses of living cholera germs at intervals of a few days, and then on removing some of the fluids from the cavity he found that something had occurred in the blood and tissues of the animal

146

which had enable it to kill and dissolve the increasing doses of the deadly germs, without the least harm to the animal itself!

By proceeding in this manner, gradually increasing the doses of the deadly germs, as the animal could support the increase without harm, Pfeiffer found that in a short time he could inject into the guinea pig, without harming it in the least, enough of the virulent cholera germs to kill one hundred ordinary guinea pigs that had not been so treated—a dose so large that only 1-100 of such dose, or even much less, would have killed the guinea pig had it been injected in the first place!

This truly interesting fact was called "Pfeiffer's phenomenon," and he first published an account of his experiments and the results in 1894 in the German Journal of Hygiene.

Immediately, over all Europe, in all the laboratories in which investigation of this kind was going on, the investigators began experiments to carry out the work of Pfeiffer, to check it, to criticize it, eternally to smash it to pieces if it were possible to do so; eternally to nail it down as true, if that were the fact. And the results swiftly verified Pfeiffer's findings; so that Pfeiffer's phenomenon took its place among the proved and accepted facts of science, with large and important effects, as you will presently see.

But Pfeiffer had done more than this. He had shown that if a small amount of the serum of such an "immunized" animal—even so small an amount that the most delicate scientific balance would be required to weigh it out, so small we might say it "amounted virtually to nothing," as the phrase has it—were injected into another ordinary guinea pig, this second guinea pig could resist without harm doses of the virulent germs which otherwise would invariably kill it. The second animal was immunized by the "immune serum" of the first.

LIVING BODY MANUFACTURES SUBSTANCES THAT PROTECT IT

Now what had occurred in the blood and the tissues of that guinea pig that caused it to be able, after a few doses of the deadly germs, to resist without feeling it a dose 100 and more times large enough to prove invariably fatal? Something surely had occurred, and that something must be this: that the presence, in ever increasing quantities, of the deadly germs in the body caused the body itself to manufacture, in ever increasing quantities, certain natural protective substances which would kill the increasing number of germs; and that these substances were either formed directly in the blood itself, or were manufactured by cells of the body and poured into the general circulation.

The guinea pig in the first place was slightly resistant to the germs—had already in its blood a little of the substance that could kill and dissolve the deadly germs. If we suppose that certain cells in the body could normally manufacture a little of that substance and cast it into the blood stream, and that the presence of increasing numbers of germs would stimulate those cells to over-activity—so that there would come to be an over-production of that substance; that there was an increasing demand for this natural resisting sub-stance which could destroy the germs by chemical action; and that this demand for over-production was promptly met by the cells of the guinea pig —why, then, we would have an explanation of Pfeiffer's phenomenon sound in every way.

That is just how the great Paul Ehrlich pro-posed to account for it, and actually did account for it with his luminous "theory of immunity" which, after 15 years or so of the fiercest kind of battering and criticism from his scientific op-ponents, who have tried every conceivable method of proving that it is wrong, is still staunch and seaworthy in all its main parts.

THESE FACTS OF IMMUNITY EXPLAIN OSTE-OPATHY'S RESULTS

You can imagine how welcome these "facts of immunity", as they are called, have proved to the osteopathic physician, who has seized them for his own, and who, by their significance, can ex-plain virtually all of the otherwise incomprehensi-ble results he gets in the treatment of germ dis-eases, and other diseases to which the theory of immunity applies.

If you can imagine that the cells of the human body normally produce a small amount of anti-poison, or anti-germ substance (just as the normal guinea pig does against cholera and typhoid), you can easily comprehend how (as in the case of the guinea pig) the cells of the human would be moved to over-production of that anti-substance when an invasion of germs takes place. But—is it not entirely probable that a certain interesting thing would occur, were the cells not able of themselves to meet the demand for over-production of the resisting substance? Is it not probable that if the blood were poured in increasing quantities (more than natural) to the affected parts, or the seat of the invasion—that if the blood were quickened more than naturally in its general circulation—that if the producing cells were indirectly stimulated by stimulation of the nerves by osteopathic methods of nerve stimulation, there would naturally follow an over-production of the resisting anti-poison far greater in amount than would follow the stimulation caused by the presence of the germs alone?

The answer is that it is not only probable, but doubtless true: for if it be not true, there is no conceivable way of accounting for the facts which are the common experience of every osteopathic physician.

I believe that if the doctors of the older school were to study the facts of immunity as they have been developed by the investigators of Europe (and the old school doctors are notably short-handed in their exact knowledge of these luminous facts), and were then to study the results of osteopathic treatment with these facts in mind, they would not be disposed to doubt the results, or what we call the "cures," effected by osteopathic treatment. For after all, it is nature—the cells and the blood—that do the work when, with the conditions not too much against him, the osteopath undertakes the treatment of disease.

Let us now return to Pfeiffer.

After Pfeiffer's publication, Gruber began a research in the effects of the serum of animals injected with typhoid germs, and found that the serum of such an animal, if mixed with living typhoid germs, would cause the germs to become motionless, and to draw together in lumps, or clumps—the phenomenon called "agglutination" (from the Greek word which means glue, or "stickiness"). But this had a tremendous effect on the diagnosis of typhoid fever in man. Pfeiffer had proved that the guinea pig injected with cholera germs was resistant in such powerful degree only against cholera—not against any other germ! The injection of cholera germs did not make it resistant to any other germ whatever. Other germs, say typhoid, would kill it in the customary doses. We therefore say that the injection of increasingly large doses of cholera germs immunizes the animal to cholera only; that the injection of increasingly large doses of typhoid germs immunizes the animal only to typhoid germs, and to no other germ whatever.

That is to say: the resisting substance which typhoid germs cause the cells of the body naturally to manufacture will be resistant only to typhoid germs; the resistance naturally manufactured by the cells in response to the injection of cholera germs is resistant only to cholera germs, and to none other. This property of the resistant substance is called its specificity—that is, it is specific for cholera or for typhoid. The substance which kills cholera germs will have no effect whatever on typhoid germs, and vice versa. In other words, each antidote, or "anti-body" manufactured naturally by the body to resist a special germ is specific for the particular germ against which it is directed. So that a guinea pig immune to cholera can easily be killed by typhoid.

HOW THE "WIDAL TEST" TO DETECT TYPHOID WORKS OUT

Now this being the case, Gruber, and also the Frenchman Widal, saw a good opportunity of using this specificity of the anti-poison to diagnose typhoid fever. For, very often, it is impossible for the physician to say whether or not his patient has typhoid fever or some other infectious disease. Sometimes it is impossible to say whether a patient has typhoid, or malaria, or even tuberculosis, or some other infectious disease, the signs of which are not always clear and positive in their pointing.

But Gruber and Widal were struck by this possibility: If the serum of an animal inoculated with typhoid germs possessed the power of causing the little rod-like germs of typhoid to be struck motionless and to stick together in lumps, or clumps (agglutination), and if this lumping, or agglutination, of typhoid germs could be caused by no serum excepting one of an animal that had been infected by the typhoid germ itself, why, then, if living typhoid were added to the serum of a patient suspected of typhoid fever and if the

152

lumping, or clumping, followed, there could be no doubt whatever that the patient was infected with typhoid fever.

The test is made in this way: A little blood is taken from the patient and the serum allowed to separate out. The serum is then diluted 25, 50, 100 and 150 times with salt solution. With a drop of each dilution is mixed a little of living typhoid germs. Then some of the germs are also mixed with a drop of bouillon, and some with a drop of plain salt solution, and all the drops are examined in the microscope. If the patient has typhoid fever, clumping of the germs takes place in drops of the patient's blood-serum that have been diluted up to 100. It does not take place in the drops of bouillon or of salt solution, which are called "controls"; that is, they control the experiment; for if the clumping occurred in the bouillon or the salt solution also, one could not be sure that the clumping was caused only by the serum of the patient. To make assurance doubly sure the test should be made with a drop of serum known to have the clumping power. Then if the clumping takes place in this drop and also in the drop of the patient's serum, and not in the drops of bouillon or salt solution, the diagnosis is sure.

OSTEOPATHY ASSISTS MAKING OF LIFE-SAVING ANTI-BODIES

Of course this is all wonderfully interesting work, and is literally one of the most remarkable and valuable contributions to human knowledge; but you must understand that its main value lies in the fact that it helps the physician to diagnose typhoid. The laboratories of our city health departments usually make the test free of charge and private laboratories make it for a fee, but it does not at all help the healer to treat or to cure typhoid fever. When the physician takes a drop of the patient's blood to test it for typhoid fever, you should know (if he does not so inform you) that the test will help him only to a knowledge of the presence or absence of the disease, and not in any manner whatever to find a cure.

The osteopath likewise uses the test (when in doubt) only to satisfy himself of the presence of the typhoid germs.

But, unlike the doctor of the old school, he does not then stand idly by and wait for nature to win or lose the momentous battle being fought in the patient's blood, but proceeds actively to assist nature, first by adjusting any existing anatomical abnormalities in the spine or elsewhere in the body (according to osteopathic technique), and if none are present, by stimulating the spinal nerves and thus energizing cells that in all probability are doing all they can to manufacture the anti-poisons which alone, by their presence in the patient's blood, destroy the germs. These natural resisting substances destroy the germs actually; and there need be no doubt that it is the increase of these substances in the patient's blood that always saves the patient's life.

There is no way known to science of making a serum that will cure typhoid fever, and this is probably so because it is necessary to kill the germs themselves. Vaccines and serums have been prepared that are claimed by some to be preventive; that is, if a person is about to be exposed to the germs these serums and vaccines are said to prevent the infection, but it is exceedingly difficult to say whether the results are positive or the reverse. These experiments, for the most part, are made upon soldiers in active army service. The general public has shown little or no disposition to submit to such experiments.

ACTUAL INVESTIGATORS PUT FORTH NO CLAIMS AS TO CURES

In no case are these claims made by any of the scientific experimenters and discoverers of the rank referred to but by the commercial pharmaceutical houses which make money out of putting forth every conceivable kind of "cures", as fast as any new theory comes out to make new experimental preparations possible. These experimental serums are urged upon the credulity of practicing physicians by relentless advertising campaigns, by glib canvassers who leave free samples and back up each new thing in turn with the most sanguine and often groundless claims for efficacy. When such serums are administered by physicians it is the solemn truth 999 times in any 1,000 chance instances that it is at the hands of those entirely unacquainted with the facts of immunity here being set forth, and, practically speaking, in no case could the physician who injects these artificially-prepared serums, taken from the bodies of the lower animals, go into the laboratory of these experimenters referred to (or others like them) and have the least knowledge of their work—the reasons, methods, technique or signification of their experiments.

So, the occasional supposed up-to-the-minute physician who injects animal serums to cure disease like typhoid and passes in his community for "an advanced man of science" really knows no more about what he is actually doing—if anything, he knows even less of what he is doing—than he did but recently when he had some special drug (or several special drugs) to prescribe in every case of disease without in the least understanding anything about drug reactions on the human body, for indeed that whole subject of drug reactions on our living bodies is not understood to this day.

If in any single disease like diphtheria there really seems to be ground to hope that antitoxin is efficacious, after hundreds of thousands of applications, the doctor who uses it is still empirical, is still "going it blind", is still experimenting, is still "practicing" upon the vitality of his patients in the strictest sense of the word. This statement of actual facts mirrors a very different state of uncertainty from what the public is generally led to believe through optimistic medical claims printed in the daily newspapers.

Actual treatment for typhoid fever is impossible, therefore, by any rational and proven means unless osteopathy be resorted to, and it is significant that osteopaths report excellent results in the treatment of this disease. The foremost medical men admit that their treatment of typhoid (and other such ills) is now drugless and is confined solely to good nursing. Osteopathy affords these cases an efficacious treatment plus good nursing.

And what is true of typhoid is true of other germ diseases.

I have spoken of typhoid simply to illustrate the general facts of the blood. These results are unquestionably due to the stimulation by osteopathic treatment of the special cells in the body (or perhaps general stimulation) which produce the substance, or substances, that destroy the germs and ultimately render the patient immune to the disease. For it is a fact that a person having recovered from typhoid (or from any other germ disease, even a common "cold") is immune to that disease for a longer or shorter time thereafter. Were such a person not immune after recovery he could never have recovered at all—such a wonderful mechanism is that mechanism called immunity.

STILL FORETOLD WHAT LATER RESEARCH HAS ESTABLISHED

Here we see again where the osteopath was on the right track for a long time without knowing the entire reason why—on the right track even before Ehrlich and Behring, Pfeiffer and Bordet, Gruber and Widal and the rest of the great European scientists had made their investigations; for you will remember that A. T. Still, M. D., founder of the osteopathic school, many years ago announced that the only cure for disease lay in the nature of the tissues and of the blood themselves. For some years now the modern, scientific osteopath has understood what he is doing, and it would pay the old school doctors to look into the osteopath's methods and theory, together with their results.

Before the revelations of laboratory investigation made it possible for the osteopath to explain the results he got, he got results notwithstanding; and in this just as in other fields, the art preceded, outran the science in its unfolding.

SCIENCE PROVES CURE OF DISEASE LIES IN BLOOD AND TISSUES

But let us figure a little on what Bordet, the Frenchman, did with the blood. Bordet, working as one of the associates of the great Metchnikoff in the Pasteur Institute at Paris, had been experimenting with cholera germs and the blood of goats, and one of his observations led him to make the following experiments: He took a little blood from a rabbit and injected it into a guinea pig. This he did three or four times. Then he bled the guinea pig, and taking some of the blood serum—the colorless fluid of the blood from which the red corpuscles had been removed—he mixed with this serum some of the red corpuscles from the blood of a rabbit. Rapidly and intensely the serum of the guinea pig dissolved the red corpuscles of the rabbit—just like the cholera germs were dissolved in "Pfeiffer's phenomenon".

Do you not see the meaning of this remarkable fact? The red blood corpuscles of the rabbit had acted as a dangerous poison to the body of the guinea pig, and the guinea pig's cells, to protect the guinea pig against the invading poisonous

blood of the rabbit, produced antidotes, or antibodies, which would promptly destroy the invaders. This protecting substance in the guinea pig's
blood had a most wonderfully destructive effect
upon the living red corpuscles of the rabbit. The
moment the rabbit's red corpuscles were mixed
with the clear serum of the guinea pig they began to dissolve—to be eaten away, as a lump of
sugar is eaten away, or dissolved, by water; and
presently, of the many millions of these minute
microscopic bi-concave straw-colored disks (called
the red corpuscles) that had been mixed with the
clear serum of the guinea pig, not one remained
intact.

Furthermore, Bordet made other experiments
by which he proved that this quickly acquired protecting power of the guinea pig's blood against the
blood of the rabbit was effective only against the
blood of the rabbit, and against the blood of no
other animal, against which the guinea pig's
serum did not have a natural solvent power. This
anti-rabbit blood power was acquired by the
guinea pig's blood only on the injection into the
guinea pig of rabbit's blood. For guinea pig's
serum will not naturally dissolve the blood cells
of the rabbit. To do so the animal must first be
injected with rabbit's blood cells.

Now this little experiment with the serum of
the little animal called the guinea pig and the
blood corpuscles of the rabbit demonstrated a fact
of tremendous value to mankind. It added another to the many practical proofs that were then
in process of accumulation, of the almost infinite

capacity of which the animal body (including the human body, of course) is possessed, not only to resist disease germs, whether they be bacteria, or the blood cells of other animals, but also to resist them and destroy them to an extent infinitely more vast than is necessary for the bare preservation of life and health! The vastness of this resisting power newly made in the body of such an animal, or of such an infected person, reminds one of the stories told by early travelers in China. When a stranger (foreign devil, the Chinese call them) would appear in a neighborhood, 5,000 or 10,000 Chinese would rush out at him to kill him, or otherwise safeguard the community from possible harm. The Chinese were taking no chances; and the body's "chemical soldiers", the anti-bodies, (as also the body's "soldier-cells", the leucocytes, of which I will speak later) act on the same principle. Foreign redblood corpuscles, or dangerous bacteria, rouse up by their presence in the body, a million times more than is necessary of the substances that destroy the particular blood corpuscles or disease germs that threaten danger.

Does not the recital of these interesting facts tend to convince you that the sole source of resistance to and cure of disease lies in the tissues and the blood themselves, and not in anything whatsover (whether drug or otherwise) that can be stuffed into the body from without? It should.

Indeed, it is these very facts which during the past twenty years have struck down the drug system of medicine, so that intelligent, up-to-date, scientifically educated doctors (and they are very few, by the way) never give drugs to their patients, excepting when the patient will not be satisfied until he or she is being fed on drugs; and even then the wise doctor of the old school hesitates, for he knows that in the end he is bound to lose his patient—in all probability to an osteopath.

It is part of the mission of the osteopath to educate the public in the discoveries that have been made (and are being made) in the great laboratories of the world in this very line of infection and immunity. For with sufficient education in this respect an intelligent public will be able to understand the osteopathic theory of treatment, and have some real knowledge of the great scientific truths of which the practical results of osteopathic therapy are the natural and logical outgrowth.

EHRLICH PROVED OUR NATURAL BLOOD RESISTANCE TO DISEASE

I wish now to say a few words about some of the things which the great Paul Ehrlich did to advance our knowledge of the blood in health and disease, for perhaps there is no one man who has done so many original and deep-reaching things as the world-renowned investigator at Frankfort. Not long ago somebody said that, were it not for Ehrlich, the world would not know any more about the blood today than it did before Ehrlich was born. That is saying a good deal, and yet it is approximately true. Not that Ehrlich found any cure for any disease, for the truth is that he did not. In German, the word Ehrlich means honest, and if there is one thing Ehrlich was he was honest. He tried to find a cure for the disease syphilis, and it was hoped he would succeed before he died, but he never made any claims for anything, nor indeed did any other of the great investigators in immunity. They do not look so much for cures as they look for facts about the conditions under which the body resists or succumbs to disease in a natural way. You must understand that neither Ehrlich nor any of these other investigators mentioned were physicians. They were all laboratory experimentalists. Their incentive was to find out the facts of the body—not to develop cures.

Ten years before this modern idea of natural resistance and natural cure for disease began to get itself a shape, Ehrlich was studying human blood and the blood of animals. The blood of animals is studied because it is as interesting to the man of science as is human blood, and its study very often enables the investigator to understand certain facts about the human blood which, if studied by themselves, would be incomprehensible. Thus we can interpret the meaning of certain facts of human blood more clearly by the study of the blood of animals than we can by the study of the human blood itself.

Ehrlich, however, spent most of his time, in those old days, in the study of human blood; and were it not for him, it would be quite impossible for the surgeon today to predict whether his patient would in all probability die of septicæmia, or blood poisoning.

In order to facilitate his understanding of the blood Ehrlich found it necessary to make a very complete study of the chemistry of numerous colors used in the dye industries. These he studied in relation to the white, or colorless, corpuscles of the blood. By using various dyes he was able to prove that there were several different species of these white corpuscles in the blood, whereas this was not known previously. The red corpuscles of the normal blood are all much the same size, and otherwise uniform, each being a slightly bi-concave disk about 8-25,000 of an inch in diameter. Of these there are about 5,000,000,000 in every 61-1,000 of a cubic inch of the blood. The leucocytes, or white corpuscles, are mostly somewhat larger, however, and there are several distinct kinds, which vary in shape, size and chemical nature. They are far less numerous, numbering only about 8,000,000 on the average in every 61-1,000 of a cubic inch of blood—a ratio of say, 8 to 5,000. Of the total number of white corpuscles about 60 to 70 per cent are the now celebrated "soldier cells", or phagocytes, of the blood, that are known to eat and destroy disease germs that enter the body.

Ehrlich, by his use of the dyes already referred to, succeeded in classifying these white corpuscles in such a way that diagnosis of disease by the blood was made possible. The white blood corpuscles (and likewise the red corpuscles) are changed by certain diseases—changed in appearance, and changed in their relative numbers—and Ehrlich did far more than any other one man to perfect the methods by which these changes are known and recognized.

Understand well that neither Ehrlich, nor any other investigator of his kind, has found, or even sought especially to find, cures for these diseases. He has found ways of identifying the disease by an examination of the blood. But that is all. When the natural tendency of the body to restore itself to the normal has won the day, the blood cells tell the story, and use is made of these facts in determining whether the patient is improving or otherwise.

Ehrlich, in addition to all this work, was the only one who could devise a theory to account for all the remarkable phenomena (and they are exceedingly numerous and highly complex) which investigators like Pfeiffer and Bordet (to say nothing of Ehrlich, who discovered many new and interesting facts of this kind, himself) found out. And the name of Ehrlich will probably remain known for many centuries as that of the most original investigator in this line that appeared at the end of the nineteenth and the beginning of the twentieth centuries.

OUR WHITE BLOOD CELLS ALSO DESTROY DISEASE GERMS

Lastly, let me recite only one discovery made by the fourth great creator of our knowledge of the blood—Metchnikoff. It was Metchnikoff who, in 1883, in the Annals of the Zoological Institute of Vienna, first announced the fact that certain white corpuscles of the blood possessed the power of engorging or eating the germs of disease, and it was for long thereafter assumed that these soldier-like cells of the blood were the only protection the body had against disease-making germs. These white corpuscles are tiny spherules, little microscopic globes of protoplasm, about 9-25,000 of an inch in diameter. A single germ of disease is very much smaller, so that the white "soldier cell" can take it in—can take several such germs into itself. The germs thus taken in (ingested, it is called) are killed by the cell, but the little soldier cell loses its own life, too, in the combat. The dead white corpuscle—killed in the defense of the body—is cast off by the body; and where great numbers of these dead white corpuscles are gathered together in an infected wound, or other infected place, they are known as pus. So, when you see pus in a wound, or other sore spot, you may know that this yellow pus is in reality millions of the dead soldier-cells that have lost their lives in the defense of your body. Isn't this highly interesting?

This was the main discovery of Metchnikoff, and surely it was worth making.

OSTEOPATHIC PRACTICE UPHELD BY ALL BIOLOGIC DISCOVERY

I have told you only a few little facts about the blood, and have tried to bring home to you the lesson that, while science has done much to ascertain the facts of health and disease, it has done next to nothing to give mankind a proportionate measure of relief. It has given us, however, the

most excellent reasons for understanding better
than ever before the solid and safe theory upon
which the practice of osteopathy is founded, not
in one of its parts, but in all; and if this lesson is
rightly taken the reader should begin to see why
osteopathy is a growing school and the ranks of
its practitioners are yearly enlarging with re-
cruits from the most intelligent and enlightened
men and women in America.

Osteopathy is the one system of treatment
which demonstrates in practice that it is able to
help and hasten these processes that prepare the
blood to rout disease. It is able in a practical way
to increase blood flow to the particular organs
that are diseased which, then more than ever, need
the healing blood stream, with its mysterious gift
of anti-bodies, potent for protection and recovery.

This, then, is the contribution which the great
Still, of America, has added to the work of his
compatriots in blood-research, of Europe, namely,
the discovery of a practical way to control and
use the circulation, through controlling the nervous system, for the practical cure of disease.
When this knowledge was applied by him as a new
form of therapeutics, he developed a complete system or science of healing called osteopathy. Now
you are in a position to understand why this system of practice is drugless. There is this additional noteworthy fact, too, that while both scientific and medical thinkers today largely devote
themselves to perfecting diagnosis to recognize
diseases but not to cure them, Still has given the
world a cure, a system of treatment that in a per-

fectly natural way helps the body to resist and overcome the agencies that make for its destruction. And this osteopathic way of purifying the living blood stream has the merit of efficiency both as a prophylaxis—that is, as a preventive of disease—and as a cure.

WHY OSTEOPATHS COMPRISE A DISTINCT PROFESSION

Thus it comes about that, while drug-school physicians, inspired by all this laboratory investigation outside the profession, have been experimenting in the hope of finding cures for all infectious diseases by the avenue of "serum therapy" —that is, by introducing into the human blood stream the serum of lower animals that has been first infected with and then immunized to these diseases—thereby going about the solution of the problem in a wholly artificial way, osteopathic investigators have approached the task from a totally different angle—in fact, from the very opposite direction, by commanding, utilizing, directing and reinforcing the recuperative resources of the body itself, and this through perfectly natural and harmless means. Happily for human welfare, they have gone a long way toward solving the problem.

By their system of manipulative therapy the osteopaths treat the human body itself. Instead of dealing with lower animals first, they treat the patient immediately and solely; they do not artificially introduce poison from lower animals into the human body, at all; but they make all needed tissue adjustments and harmonize all the opera-

tions of the human organism so that without let
or hindrance it may be able to prepare its own
natural defensive substances as needed; and, then,
further, by their art of stimulating the body's
cells through work upon the nervous system—
which in response demonstrates the mysterious
power of releasing increase of cell energy wherever this stimulation is applied—they enable the
body in a practical way to manufacture its own
anti-bodies, or contra-poisons, or antidotes which
rout the disease germs, thus causing recovery
from the disease.

Discovering, as Still did, that this was possible in a thoroughly practical way—when confined
to the hands of practitioners trained in his method
of observation, reasoning and technique—constitutes one of the gigantic achievements of the human mind when measured by its power for good
to the human species.

This discovery—that the forces of the body may
be applied by the trained physician through intelligent manipulation—was made one of the foundation stones of osteopathic science; and it early
revealed the necessity of developing a new and
distinct profession with a differently trained body
of practitioners who would apply these fundamental facts of science to the care of the body
in a wholly new and revolutionary manner.
Hence the practice of osteopathy as it is known
today.

Of course in a brief popular discussion you will
appreciate that it is only possible to present some
one aspect of a subject as profound and complex
as osteopathy and the group of underlying sci-

ences on which it is based. No doubt there arises at this moment a number of questions you would like to ask about these matters to bridge the gap of your present knowledge. I wish there were opportunity to anticipate your perplexities here. You surely cannot as yet hold very clear or adequate conception of what osteopathy is and does and how it does it if your knowledge of the subject is confined to what you learn in such a brief presentation. But what you have considered is fundamental, and without understanding these matters somewhat you never could have any real insight into all the wonderful things which are taking place in the body whenever an osteopath treats his patient. Now you have a glimmering of it—and in other chapters I have endeavored to tell the story in a different way, easy to understand if you keep these main facts in mind that you have learned about the body's twin mysteries of immunity and infection.

CHAPTER IX

BODY CHEMISTRY, GERMS AND OSTEOPATHY

The remarkable success which osteopathic physicians have had with germ diseases is often a cause of wonder and surprise to the patients, and to the families of patients who have applied to the osteopath for treatment. It will be a matter of interest to the general public to explain in as simple a way as possible the reasons for osteopathic success in diseases known to be caused by germs or, at least, to be associated with germs. These diseases are called "infectious" diseases, or "germ diseases", and we will consider some of them here.

To explain the facts to the lay reader it is necessary to depart a little from the subject of infectious diseases itself, and to state that osteopathic success in these diseases is due altogether to a great fact in Nature—the great natural fact—demonstrated by science—that the living body is truly and completely in its entire structure and function a matter of chemical composition and chemical reaction.

To say that the body is nothing but a great chemical fact may sound strange to those who are unfamiliar with physiology. But such is the truth. Physiological chemists are special chemists who study and experiment with the tissues of the body;

who analyze the body; who discover the various substances of which the body is built up. And physiologists are men who try to discover how these various substances act in the living body. The difference between a living body and a dead body is believed by physiologists and by chemists to consist in the different conduct of these substances in the two cases. This is not absolutely proved as yet, but scientists believe it is so. The dead body no longer takes into itself substances from the outside which it builds up into its own substance (food) nor does it throw off the products of its living energy, such as come from it in the form of carbonic acid from the lungs, water from the sweat glands, and numerous chemical substances found in the excretion from the kidneys.

Now all this is very intimately associated with the frightful disturbance the body passes through when, owing to some defect or fault in the body itself, it is invaded by germs—by disease-making bacteria. And we will ask the reader to follow us a little way into this chemistry of the body before considering its intimate relation with osteopathic treatment and success. Osteopathy is first and foremost founded on scientific fact. Some of these facts we will now point out.

THE CHEMISTRY OF THE LIVING BODY

A little—a very little—study of chemistry will teach us that all things in existence—all the things we can see, and all the things we cannot see, from the globe of the earth with its vast envelopes of water and air, from the sun and the stars, down to the microscopic particle of less than 4-10,000 of an inch in diameter, are merely chemical compounds, or chemical elements of which chemical compounds consist. The great meteor that falls out of the sky is pure iron. Iron is a chemical element. Pure iron never occurs on the earth, but has to be separated from some other element with which it is found united. Hematite ore, for example, is iron chemically combined with oxygen. Now oxygen is another element, but oxygen is a gas. When the two elements are in chemical union they form the beautiful many-colored hematite ore, mined in enormous quantities in the Great Lakes mining region. The ore is taken to the reduction plant, the oxygen is driven off, and we thus have the pure iron of industry.

Now the air around us consists of one-fifth oxygen and four-fifths nitrogen—another gaseous element. Iron and oxygen combine together in chemical union, forming iron oxide in nature, and iron combined in other natural ways is found in the bodies of all animals and plants. The liver carries a great store, or stock of iron; iron enters into the chemical composition of the red blood corpuscles—the little bodies that give the blood its red color; and iron is a constituent of every one of those microscopic little units of the body which we call cells. Oxygen also enters very largely into the chemical compounds of which the body consists. Without the oxygen we draw into our blood through the lungs we could not live an hour. Without oxygen the body could not use at all the food it takes into itself. Without oxygen we should die of asphyxiation. Even when the lungs of an animal are collapsed by opening the air-tight cavity in which they naturally expand and contract by the movements of the muscles of respiration, the animal while perfectly unconscious, will make the most distressing and convulsive efforts to breathe, so that an observer would be convinced it were consciously trying to "get its breath"—so necessary to life are the chemical compounds in which oxygen enters. All the elements that enter into the compounds of which the body consists are familiar to us in the material of which the earth is made. Sodium and chlorine which, when combined, make sodium chloride—common table salt —are found in almost all the fluids of the body. Calcium and phosphorus are found in the bones as calcium phosphate; carbon and oxygen unite in the body as carbonic acid, and these two elements, together with hydrogen, nitrogen, phosphorus and sulphur, unite together to form the wonderful chemical "compound" of which living matter essentially consists. This compound is called protoplasm (and dead protoplasm is called protein) and is distinguished from the other compounds of the body by the peculiar manner in which its nitrogen is united with the other elements of carbon, oxygen, phosphorus and sulphur. About 70 per cent of the body's weight consists of water, and water is a compound of the two gases, hydrogen and oxygen. A biological architect who knew the necessary chemistry — we might easily imagine — could take some twelve or fewer elements, including those above mentioned, and build with them a living animal. This, of course, is from the viewpoint of the cold-blooded chemist.

Now these wonderfully complex compounds of which the body consists are distributed in the body in the form of what are called "tissues". The different tissues are chemically different from one another. The secreting organs, like the stomach, the liver, the kidneys, the intestines, the pancreas, the salivary glands, the thyroid gland, and others, each produces its own chemical product. The gastric juice is the chemical product of that chemical factory, the stomach. The liver manufactures we do not know how many different chemical products. The liver manufactures urea and throws it into the blood to be taken out in the urine by the kidneys. The liver destroys uric acid. The liver manufactures a mysterious chemical substance which converts glucose-sugar, the form in which sugar appears in the body, into a substance very like starch; and stores this substance in the liver tissue; and the liver makes another mysterious chemical compound which again reconverts this animal starch into glucose-sugar and throws it back again into the blood. Were the liver to lose its control over sugar (sugar as a chemical compound consisting of carbon, hydrogen and oxygen) there would be an end of life.

But these are only a few examples. All that goes on in the body is chemical, and the most complex, delicately equilibrated kind of chemism: so that you can easily understand why nothing that will interfere with these numerous delicate reactions should be allowed to enter the body.

In chemistry we have what are called active and inert substances. An active substance is one which causes a chemical change in the substance to which it is added. An inert substance is one which causes no such change. Were you to chew up and swallow a fist full of white paper, or swallow a handful of pebbles or a cupful of bran, these substances would cause no chemical change in your body, but would pass out of it unaltered. They are inert substances in the body. They are neither food nor poison. Food and poison are both active substances. They cause chemical change in the body, and are chemically changed themselves.

Now physiologists assert that all active substances which are not foods are poisons. And the word of the physiologist may be accepted as true. It is a knowledge of this great fact of physiology that is causing the widespread and popular reaction against the use of the old-style drastic and poisonous drugs which the intelligent physician now hesitates to prescribe—preferring rather to let "Nature take its course"—and which the intelligent patient hesitates to swallow. These facts account for the increasing success of the osteopathic physician and for the growing use of osteopathy among the most intelligent and enlightened classes of patients. Osteopathic physicians have long since learned to take their success calmly and as a matter of course, knowing full well that their success is due altogether to the fact that osteopathy is founded on the well-known and scientifically proved facts of the body's life.

The osteopathic physican not only agrees with the physiologist in the physiologists's chemical view of the body and administers no active drugs, but he goes farther. He uses the chemistry that is natural to the body to restore to the body the very chemical equilibrium which the body, through whatever fault or defect, has lost. Under his fingers he has the wonderful keyboard of the nervous system, with its nerve fibers communicating directly or indirectly with every minute part and cell of the body, and under the normalizing impulse thus given, the organs and parts of the body that are out of chemical equilibrium leap in response. No active drug is needed to hasten or retard the marvelous work going on in these chemical factories. The nerve is the "master tissue" and the other tissues are its slaves. The osteopath controls the nerves. That is the secret.

NATURAL CONTROL OF THE BODY'S CHEMISTRY

When you see a nerve cell under the microscope, it looks like some vast gray-colored water animal with numerous exquisitely sensitive tentacles reaching out in many directions, one of which is prolonged enormously. This long tentacle is the nerve fibre, and many thousands, or tens of thousands, or millions of these fibres make up the nerve, or nerve trunk. All the muscles, all the glands, all the other organs and parts of the body are the mere slaves of these microscopic, monster-like organisms, the nerve cells. The osteopath sends his message to the disordered organ or part through these masters of the body, and the message brings blood to the part or bids the blood flow from the part precisely as the case requires, either to stimulate or normalize the organ to its own peculiar activity.

Every organ, every part of the body, has its own corresponding place on the marvelous keyboard of the flexuous spinal column, and instantaneously the osteopath reaches the disordered part by manipulating the nerve fibres that control its chemism. It is like the operation of a telephone exchange in perfect order. That is the reason why osteopaths have had such splendid success in the treatment of the fifty or more alleged diseases of the stomach and heart.

Many patients have suffered death a thousand times over from "heart diseases" diagnosed as "stomach troubles". It was really the heart—not the stomach. And the osteopath has cured such diseases by his intelligent, scientific understanding of the nerve centers by which the heart is controlled. The heart and the stomach are tied up together by the same nerve—the great vagus or pneumogastric nerve. Hold a glass of water to your mouth with your left hand, and put your finger to the pulse of your left hand then swallow —not too fast—the water in the glass, and note how your pulse changes the rhythm of its beats. Do that, and you will have the key to the fact why the osteopath—understanding the connection between the chemistry of the body and its nerves —administers the only treatment that science can endorse, and cures his patient in Nature's own way.

Osteopaths have been highly pleased by the success they have had in treating diseases due to bacteria or germs. Each day we learn a little more about germ diseases and germs. Bacteria harmful to men get into the body through a lowering of its resistance, and by their multiplication in the body produce certain chemical substances poisonous to the tissues. These poisons, or "toxins", as we call them, are chemical compounds which destroy the tissues, or which disturb the great chemical factories of the body in the normal manufacture of their products. When these disease-making germs find an entrance into a body susceptible to them they grow with unthinkable rapidity and the body puts forth both its white-blood cells and its entire chemical force fighting them. We assert with positive truth that there is no medical treatment given to fight the germs which will not hurt a patient suffering from one of these diseases.

The osteopath, like the doctors of the old school, studies the science of bacteriology, and in these studies he, as well as the modernly-educated doctor of the old school, has been taught that there is no "medicine" which can fight the germs. The only substance which can be taken by the sufferer from a germ disease that will help him in Nature's battle against the invaders is nourishing food. Possibly some harmless substance (in reality a food, such as castor oil), or soap-enemas administered to quicken, when expedient, the emptying of the intestines, may be a helpful thing as medical treatment; but you should realize that osteopathy by its own independent treatment secures the unloading of the bowels without the use of any purgative whatsoever. (Osteopaths, of course, use enemas freely.)

THE BODY MAKES ITS OWN MEDICINES

Germ diseases such as typhoid fever, certain other forms of intestinal disorders such as "running from the bowels", bloody dysentery, various disorders of the stomach, "common colds", bronchitis, spinal fever, scarlet fever, tonsillitis, grip or influenza, diphtheria and other infections which will be mentioned hereafter, can be and are relieved and often completely stopped by osteopathic treatment, because of the fact that the only cure possible in these cases is the chemical resistance of the body to the germs and their poisons. The body is already fighting with all its power to overcome the destructive effects of the germs. With every beat of the heart the blood is sent through all the tissues bearing countless billions of its devouring white-blood cells (phagocytes) and its newly made chemical soldiers (antitoxins) to neutralize the poisons of the germs and to destroy the germs themselves. This is Nature's own work, and if the body is not naturally strong enough to win the fight—if it is destined to lose the battle—it quits the struggle only in the last ditch.

Now the question is this: Can the body be helped in this struggle with the bacteria? It matters little whether the germ disease be an actual pneumonia or other rapidly destructive invasion of germs, or whether it be a "simple cold" (which is often easily conquered by the blood, but which too often, when neglected, finishes in pneumonia or tuberculosis). The only difference between the way the body fights pneumonia, diphtheria, influenza, chronic catarrh, or any other germ disease—even scarlet fever or smallpox, or the plague or yellow fever—and the way it fights a "simple cold" is this: that in the "simple cold" the body quickly produces, first, a great army of white-blood cells, and, second, a great chemical army of Nature's own anti-toxins which by their numbers overwhelm both the invading germs and the toxins made by them. In the other diseases, and in cases where the "simple cold" paves the way for the development of pneumonia or tubercular bronchitis, the "reaction" of the body to the germ-poisons is slower and of less extent. The body cannot produce its army of phagocytes and natural anti-toxins or germ fighters quickly enough, or in sufficient number, to destroy the germs and their poisons. "Medicine" in these cases is no longer prescribed. But right here is where the osteopathic physician steps in and helps Nature when Nature can be helped in no other way. How does he do it?

OSTEOPATHIC ADJUSTMENT SAVES THE DAY

The osteopathic physician claims and proves that scientific and intelligent adjustment, stimulation or normalization (as the case requires) of spinal tissues (not massage or the ignorant manipulations of untrained and unscientific hands, but genuine osteopathic adjustment) will increase the activity of the organs the cells of which manufacture the chemical soldiers that overcome the poisons of the invading germs. In a word the body manufactures natural anti-toxins. This has been proved so often in pneumonia, in typhoid, in grip, in tonsillitis, in diphtheria, in cerebro-spinal meningitis, and in other virulent germ diseases that it is now a commonplace fact of osteopathic practice which, as I have said before, is taken by the osteopath and his patients as a matter of course. The osteopath knows this fact well, and he knows, furthermore, that if the body can make a reasonably strong effort in raising its army, he, with his ready and prompt assistance, can reinforce it by using the great master tissue, the nerves, on the body cells and the blood to spur on—to help forward—the process of resistance. And this fact is attested today by thousands of families in which the osteopath has been called early and late in these diseases.

HOW OSTEOPATHS GIVE POWER TO THE HEART

The osteopath, too, is a powerful factor in sustaining the heart by natural stimulation when, in the destructive germ disease, it has been weakened and battered by the toxins of the germs. This kind of heart support is a thousand times more rational than the use of powerful drugs which the intelligent medical man of today hates—yea, trembles to use, but which, unfortunately, he often feels compelled to use, knowing no other way, rather than see the patient die under his hands. And the most alarming consideration is the terrific after-effects of these drugs on the heart— weeks, months or years later—which account for most of the sudden deaths from so-called modern "heart failure" among patients that have been so treated. From the natural (and powerful) osteopathic stimulation of the heart there is no quick and dangerous reaction—there is no reaction at all, nor later disaster, as is the case with the pharmacological stimulants and regulators, for, by giving the organ a more adequate blood supply, it is furnished with greater stores of the fuel which it uses up in doing its normal work, and hence the heart is permanently strengthened, not weakened, by osteopathic treatment.

Then, too, the osteopath controls the heart with much of the assurance with which one can work the handle of a pump—fast or slow, weak or strong, as the case demands.

So that in germ diseases the intelligent layman, with these facts in mind, will easily comprehend the reason why osteopathic treatment is the rational treatment indicated by Nature itself.

OSTEOPATHY FIGHTS ON THE SIDE OF NATURE

Again in chronic bronchitis when not caused by germs, but by heart lesions, or by displacement of joints in the spine or ribs (a common occurrence), the disease can be vastly relieved by imparting muscle "tone" to the heart and to the rest of the body, or in the second category of cases it can be removed altogether by correcting the bony displacement according to osteopathic technique.

The osteopath claims and proves that normalization and stimulation of the spinal tissues can and does assist the patient's body in overcoming the effects of the bacterial invasion. He stimulates the heart, as just explained, by Nature's own stimulant—the nerve. While he observes all the required precautions in the way of adequate and suitable nourishment, careful nursing, sanitary measures, and the other aspects of regimen which common sense and experience indicate as useful, he does bring in the help which the bacteriologist with sorrow deplores as non-existent. The bacteriologist is speaking honestly, and with the highest and best motives, when he says that "in the battle between the germ and the body, all we can do is to watch with intense interest the ultimate outcome". Yet the bacteriologist in good time will learn that osteopathy has found a way of taking an active part in the battle, and reinforcing the body with its own chemical troops which, if they do not always decide the day, at least decide it many, many times.

SCIENTIFIC MEN NEVER TAKE DRUGS THEMSELVES

The harmful effect of drugs on the living body has been long known and realized by the really scientific man, such as the bacteriologist, the physiologist, the chemist and the pharmacologist. Men like these who, knowing that drugs were worse than useless, began a few years ago to investigate germ diseases with the hope of finding, in the germs themselves, some hidden cure for the diseases which the germs produced. This was the beginning of what is now known as "serum therapy". It consists in the injection into the human body of the liquid part of the blood—that is, the part of the blood that remains after the clot has been removed—of an animal that has been treated with the germs which produce the special disease that it is desired to cure.

Now in justice to the men who have been experimenting in the laboratories with serum therapy, it is only fair to say that they have made no great claims whatever for this method of treatment! Rash and over-zealous doctors have hailed the mere hopes of the experimenters as actual discoveries, and sensational newspapers have grossly exaggerated the optimistic claims of the rash doctors; but conservative doctors are always very cautious in the use of new and dangerous agents which may work more harm than good.

Commercial drug houses have put on the market all sorts of useless and even harmful preparations, and have tried hard to induce doctors to use them by shamelessly exaggerated claims of their virtues, but few intelligent physicians are caught in the trap. The most conservative men in the world, however, with regard to the power of serum therapy are the original discoverers themselves. They know the limitations and the extreme dangers of the method, and have long since come to the conclusion that science must look in other directions for a rational and safe method of fighting germs in the bodies of men.

THE GREAT EHRLICH ABANDONED SERUM "CURES"

The greatest genius of experimental therapy in the world—so acclaimed at the recent International Medical Congress at London—I mean Professor Ehrlich, of Frankfort-am-Main—before his death abandoned serum work, regarding the field as already worked out, and in his last work devoted himself exclusively to the study of the effects of certain chemical compounds on the germ of syphilis. Such things are highly significant.

But, out of all this study and investigation of the chemistry of serums have come many great truths, the greatest of which is this: the only germ destroyer which can be depended upon, and the only germ destroyer that will not injure the body of the patient, is the blood and tissues of the patient himself!

This fact—now announced from the scientific laboratories of the world as the highest generalization of modern pathology—was taught as a fundamental truth of osteopathy by Still twenty-five years before the science of experimental pathology was born! This announcement of Still's—which is today regarded as an almost self-evident axiom of experimental pathology—could not have been understood by the best pathologists of his day, and it could not be understood simply because the knowledge and experimental proof of the luminous facts of this young science were still locked up in the treasury of the future.

OSTEOPATHS AS RESEARCHERS OF THE LIVING BODY

So that the osteopathic practitioner is justified in feeling that for all these years, while the laboratory researchers toiled to vindicate and verify the supreme intuition of the founder of osteopathy, he himself has been traveling the safe and solid highway which the experimental pathologists were yet in the process of building or even of shaping the stones that were laid down. Accept-

ing Still's theory as true, the osteopathic physician, by the quick and positive results flowing
from the subtle touches of his finger tips on the
living body, has been and is a living and daily
verifier and demonstrator of a therapeutic theory
which is still twenty years in advance of ordinary
medical thinking.

This, then, is the great and beautiful discovery
that has been made and established as an absolute fact by the wonderful experiments of the research men in Europe. Their work has proved,
once and forever, that the only cure for disease
is the cure which Nature has already installed in
the body. And many of the foremost leaders in
this work besides Professor Ehrlich have abandoned serum therapy as a futile hope for man,
while a great many others never had any faith in
it at all. They are still studying the blood and its
conduct in abnormal conditions. This new science
is called "Experimental Pathology" and those who
are working in it are in reality working along
osteopathic lines.

THE LITTLE LEFT TO SERUM THERAPY

Serum therapy—that is serums offered as
"cures"—is regarded by osteopathic physicians
with open minds. They await more complete evidence. As among other schools of practice,
there is wide divergence of opinion as to how
much or how little ground there is for the tremendous claims made for it by those who advocate its
use. Certain it is that only a small fraction of
truth, as weighed by the evidence, is to be found
in the wild and sensational claims made by the

daily press for the several serums still being experimented with; and unfortunately the desire to make good newspaper "copy" seems entirely to outweigh the desire of the press to get at the real scientific facts. Such doctors as are uneducated greatly encourage these fanciful claims but, as I have stated, the experimenters themselves as a class are very skeptical regarding serum "cures" while well-educated physicians almost all share this conservatism of view very fully.

But the osteopath positively asserts—even granting for the sake of argument that the use of the serum therapy may arrest the destruction produced by bacteria in two or three certain diseases only—that osteopathic treatment without serums scores a higher percentage of real cures, not the sort of "recoveries" which show a later train of serious or fatal retributions due to mistaken ideas of therapy. Following the use of serums in countless patients that have been left in a deplorable condition as a result of administering these much-praised but oft-failing "cures", osteopathy works many actual and complete cures. For example: it has cured the paralysis of many children resulting from and following the antitoxin treatment of diphtheria.

The entire claims of results of all the work that has been done in serum are now limited strictly to (1) diphtheria serum: (2) the supposed reduction of mortality in spinal fever by the Flexner serum: (3) the beneficial results in a small number of cases of boils and acne (pimples) by Wright's vaccines: (4) the new "immunity treat-

ment" for typhoid now under experiment by the
U. S. Army; (5) the ancient and much disputed
questionable use of vaccination in smallpox: (6)
a preventive (not curative) serum for tetanus:
and (7) the hydrophobia treatment. This sum-
mary includes the sum total of the fruit of all the
incalculable mass of research work done in the
hope of curing disease by these methods. The
possibilities of serum and vaccine therapy have
been considered for some time past by the foremost workers and critics of the European laboratories as having been completely exhausted. Serum therapy will probably rest on the laurels it
has already won, such as they are.

The great science of pathological physiology, or
experimental pathology, has now largely dropped
"serum cures" as being perfectly impossible in
virtually all but the few diseases named and is
now turning its attention in other directions.
Therefore, the popular notion, derived from Sun-
day newspapers, that serum therapy has a "great
future" before it, has really never been believed
by the best experts who have delved in this field.
They look upon serum therapy as a worked out
mine.

INFANTILE PARALYSIS

Spinal meningitis, or spinal fever, or infantile
paralysis—that dread disease of the young—is a
disease which osteopathy can reach through the
blood when it can be reached at all. If Nature has
left in the body the slightest tendency to fight this
disease—as is usually the case—osteopathy can
help the fight along by pouring the blood in more

generous quantities to the tissue where the battle is being fought. Osteopaths have had success in this dread disease where the medical practitioner has thrown up his hands. Given a fighting chance, the body of the patient tends to conquer the germs itself. And with this fighting chance on his side, the osteopath has a tremendous advantage over the ordinary practitioner because the latter is a mere spectator of the battle while the osteopath directly and indirectly assists Nature in the resisting process already begun.

RHEUMATISM

Another germ disease which osteopathy can influence is the more common one of rheumatism. Rheumatism is supposed to be due to a germ as yet little known, nor has this germ been positively identified. But it is a fact that in rheumatic patients the body is always putting up a splendid chemical fight, which should not be interfered with by the administration of useless and harmful drugs.

Of course, if a rheumatic patient will further insist on using alcohol and tobacco—two of the most active drug-poisons known to men—osteopathy cannot miraculously overcome the effect of these poisons in rheumatism. If the rheumatic patient who puts himself under the care of an osteopath wisely refrains from these two pronounced aggravators of the disease, osteopathy can help him. This treatment for rheumatism is the only treatment that has accomplished practical results. Old rheumatic patients are always agreeably surprised by the results of osteopathic

treatment, nor should the newly attacked neglect
this sole chance that is offered them of assisting
their blood and their tissues in the eternal battle
against the germs.

In other diseases due to germs, osteopathy has
more than demonstrated its usefulness. Germs
hurtful to man get into the intestines, or the blood
of the man fails in its chemical constituents in
such a way that harmful germs already in the intestines are permitted to multiply. The large intestine is infested with bacteria which ordinarily
are not harmful. More than fifty different kinds
of germs have their abiding place in the gut.
When human stools—that is, the daily output of
the intestines—are dried and examined, it is found
that one-third of their weight consist of bacteria.
This is a tremendous proportion.

Now under certain conditions some of these
germs—either normal or not to the intestine—
multiply and cause many sorts of trouble. Inflammation of the large intestine (colitis), putrefaction of lean meat, temporary or chronic diarrhoea,
and appendicitis (or some of the numerous forms
of miscnief called appendicitis, in which the appendix is involved), typhlitis or inflammation of
the blind end of the large intestine from which
the appendix comes off as a blind sac, and other
bacterial intestinal disturbances, are germ diseases which osteopathy can help, or cure, providing that reasonable measures be taken in the diet-
ary habits of the patient so that the patient will
not be continually counteracting the treatment.
In intestinal putrefaction, so-called "auto-intoxi-

cation", the patient should not eat much meat, as that error overcomes the effects of the increased circulation which osteopathic treatment sends to the intestine: it is deliberately a case of feeding the bacteria with the food that produces the poison. In this case the undigested meat acts like a drug and is a poison. But when this occurs the patient will do well to follow the counsel and advice of the osteopathic physician who knows quite well what his patient needs in the way of food, and, when necessary, restricts the diet to vegetables.

In other cases of intestinal bacterial disease the contrary is necessary. The patient needs solid meat for his diet and should have it: for lean meat (except in a few cases) supplies to the blood and the tissues the chemical substances which help the body to fight the invading germs. Many an osteopath has made well men out of patients who, with slight nervous disorders of the stomach, have failed to find relief, either in the regulation of diet or in the stomach tonics of the old therapeutics. It is said that fifty per cent of all the patients who seek treatment are suffering from disorders that originally rise in the great digestive tract. This is probably true, and there would be fewer sick men in the world if the sufferer, when he first feels the discomforts of disorder in the stomach and intestines, would have them corrected by forestalling the bacteria through prompt osteopathic measures.

In men—especially older men—the bladder and the prostate gland are the seat of much discomfort

191

which may or may not be caused by germs. The old way of treating these male disorders is to hand the poor man a prescription which, by disturbing the chemistry of his stomach, makes his original discomfort worse. Osteopathic treatment is required here if anywhere. I have in mind a special case within my own knowledge in which the man under the drug treatment was contemplating a business failure (he is a large manufacturer) by reason of his inability to look after his interests. Three months' treatment by an osteopath restored him to his work and although that was four years ago he has never been near a doctor since—not even an osteopathic doctor.

MALARIAL FEVER

Another type of germ diseases that are specially amenable to osteopathic treatment are the fevers that are called "autumnal" (malarial fever). Malarial fever is due to the multiplication in the blood of an animal parasite which destroys the red blood corpuscles. The body strives to overcome the parasites—to kill them—by the development of anti-poisons, while at the same time it replaces the destroyed corpuscles by over-activity in the red bone marrow where the red corpuscles are made. Osteopathic treatment here is of special value not only in helping the body in its natural fight, but in helping it to throw off future attacks by quickly destroying the new host of invaders.

CHAPTER X

OSTEOPATHY POTENT WHERE
SERUMS AND VACCINES
FAIL

Whether you are healthy or sick, whether young or old, whether rich or poor, whatever be your profession, station, or reputation, you are interested in the subject of infectious diseases, because all individuals, from the ruler of a nation and the multi-millionaire to the humblest and poorest person in the world, is liable at any moment to fall a victim to one of the diseases that, in the form of microscopic germs, is making ill or is killing some brother man.

The Apostle Paul truly says that no man liveth to himself, no man dieth to himself alone, but all men live and die together, and the millionaire's baby, as well as the millionaire himself, may be killed by the disease germ coming from the mouth of the most lowly and oppressed laborer or laborer's child in his own tenement or factory. To enlarge on these facts is the purpose of the present chapter.

Year after year the good results which follow osteopathic treatment in infectious diseases have attracted increasing attention from the osteopathic profession, and have been so highly favorable that it would certainly seem that this treatment, especially when it is given early in the course of the infection, is in reality a specific for the diseases in question. In a recent number of this magazine we spoke in detail of the remarkable results that follow osteopathic treatment in influenza, popularly called la grippe, or the grip. We have now to dwell further on certain peculiar phases of osteopathy when used for treatment of other or generally infectious diseases, and to lay before the reader certain interesting facts in addition to those written about in that recent number. These facts and their interpretation are valuable as a general contribution to the campaign of education in health and disease that is now being carried on universally by the popular magazines, the newspapers, and thru them by the various state and city health departments of the country, by the social settlements and by organized work in the public schools.

It should be explained that it is not scientifically correct to say that osteopathy is a specific for any particular infection, because that would mean that osteopathy is not a remedy for any other disease but the one in question. What is meant is that osteopathy acts in many infections as an ideal specific would act were such a specific remedy in existence. How far such remedies do exist we shall undertake to show in the present paper, while showing, at the same time, a peculiar and interesting parallel between osteopathy and certain facts in the results of scientific investigation in infectious diseases and natural and acquired immunity to them.

An infectious disease is any disease acquired thru the entrance into the body tissues of certain destructive agents, all of which are living organisms, either of the plant kind or of the animal kind, all of which multiply with great rapidity, once they find lodgement in the body, and all of which are so very minute that they can not be seen excepting in high powers of the microscope. Of these disease-producing organisms there are in the neighborhood of thirty. Some of these "germs" or "micro-organisms" as they are called, in their growth and multiplication secrete substances that are more or less toxic, or poisonous, to the body and destroy the tissues of the body— on a large scale, if the organism be virulent, on a smaller scale if it be less virulent, or milder. The secretion of some of these organisms, on the other hand, are so mild (innocuous) in the body as to be scarcely worthy of the name toxin, or poison, but these germs are none the less deadly. In fact, the least virulent germs oftentimes are accompanied by the most extensive and deep-seated destruction of body organs and cause the most stubborn diseases, as does the tubercular bacillus.

The destruction is not caused by the germ itself or its toxin but by the attempt of the body to overcome the germ—what pathologists call the reaction of the body against the invading organism. All these germs, virulent and not, are called "pathogenic organisms", whether of the plant kind or the animal kind; pathogenic because they produce disease. In order to understand how osteopathy works in these diseases, it is needful to study a

195

little the germs themselves—or some few types of the germs—and the diseases they cause; to study rather how the body tries to overcome the germs and their toxins.

Micro-organisms, as we have seen, are either plant forms or animal forms. Organisms called bacteria belong to the lowest forms of plant life, and the simplest forms of animal life are called protozoa. Of these low forms of plant and animal life many hundreds of kinds are known, but only a few—say about thirty—are harmful to man. Some few other kinds are harmful to the lower animals and not to man; some of those that are harmful to man are harmless for the lower animals, and some of the pathogenic germs are harmful to man and lower animals both. These varied facts have made it possible for bacteriologists to experiment on animals with germs that are also injurious to man, and artificially to reproduce in animals diseases which are common in man and study the beginnings, the progress and the termination of these diseases (and many other facts) at their leisure and under conditions impossible when the diseases are found in the human body.

Most of the infectious diseases commonly familiar are caused by bacteria—organisms of the plant kingdom; while only a few of the infectious diseases are caused by micro-organisms of the animal kingdom. Smallpox and syphilis are the most common diseases caused by animal organisms. Until very recently, it was believed that typhus fever and scarlet fever were caused by animal organisms, but it has now been shown that the invading organisms in these two diseases are bacteria, a bacillus in both cases. Bacteria are mainly of two kinds—cocci (minute spherical organisms) and bacilli (minute rod-like organisms). There are many different cocci as well as many different bacilli, and only about twenty-five of these produce disease in the human body, the others being harmless.

DIFFERENCE BETWEEN INFECTIOUS AND CONTAGIOUS DISEASES

It is desirable to explain what infectious and contagious diseases are; rather what is sought to be conveyed by these two terms. When we say a disease is infectious we mean it is caused by one of the pathogenic germs that has invaded the body and is growing there. When we say a disease is contagious we mean that the germ causing it is readily and easily passed on from the person infected to other persons. Therefore, it would appear that all contagious diseases are infectious also, but that all infectious diseases are not necessarily contagious. This used to be the general opinion. But in recent years the confusion in this matter of infectious and contagious diseases has been slowly cleared up. All contagious diseases are infectious, but all infectious diseases are also contagious—for some persons. A non-contagious disease is caused by a germ—bacterium or animal organism — that is easily passed around. That is to say if numerous persons in a community are highly susceptible to the particular germ, numerous persons will take the germ in and it will grow in them. But it would seem to be clear that the extent of the infection (contagion in this case) will depend upon two things: first, the susceptibility of numerous persons in the community, and secondly, the method by which the germ is passed around.

Now contagion means contact, but contact can only mean contact with the germ, whether that contact is encompassed by actual touch with the infected person's body (and hence with the germ in that body) or contact apart from the person's body—the germ having been scattered about by the infected person in one or another way.

There is, therefore, in fact, no real distinction between infection and contagion. If all but a few persons in a community are immune to a germ, such a germ may be brought into contact with such persons—they may actually take it in—but it will not grow in their tissues, and the disease can not be called contagious, in the old meaning of the word. Few persons in the world are susceptible to leprosy. Therefore, this disease, which was regarded as contagious, is now no longer regarded so. Contact with lepers (or with the germ) causes the disease only in an insignificant few. Bacteriologists in recent times have come to believe that all disease-making germs must be passed directly from person to person; that few if any infections—tuberculosis, pneumonia, la grippe and so on—are carried in the air or food. Close proximity to the infected person is believed to be necessary, the germ being coughed or sneezed out and directly taken in by the new victim's nose or mouth. Again germs are transmitted by animals from man to man; by flies, mosquitoes, and perhaps dogs, cats, and directly from rats to fleas, and by fleas to man, as in the bubonic plague; or by lice, as in typhus and relapsing fever. The sleeping sickness is caused by a microscopic animal organism that is conveyed by the bite of an African fly; malaria, as is well known, by a microscopic parasite transmitted from man to man by the bite of the mosquito; also, in a similar manner is yellow fever passed about among men. Scarlet fever is passed to others in the nasal and throat secretion of the patient, and the same is probably true of smallpox. Sneezing and coughing out invisible droplets of germ-laden saliva, and the taking in of these droplets into the nose and mouth of others, while the germs are yet alive, cause most of the pneumonia and tuberculosis we see around us. Kissing is the indirect cause of we do not know how many cases of pneumonia, tuberculosis, and la grippe. Unclean habits have probably more to do with the passing about of typhoid fever than polluted water supply. As long as men are herded together like cattle in the cities and the other cattle pens of industry (men ignorant of such facts as these) the world will always be threatened with infectious diseases, or remain actual victims of them. The only reason that boils and "blood poisoning" are not as common as hunger is because only a few persons per 100,000 are susceptible to the staphylococcus pyogenes aureus, and to the streptococcus pyogenes—two insignificant invisible plant organisms—bacteria—of the lowest and simplest forms of living things.

Another interesting fact about infectious disease is this: Only one kind of germ may be the cause of several different diseases so called, depending upon the location in the body where the germ chances to be growing. Thus colon bacillus may cause abscesses in the bladder, the kidney, or in other parts of the body; pneumococcus may cause bladder disease, pneumonia, or a "cold" and its toxin may cause death from kidney disease; streptococcus pyogenes may cause tonsillitis, and spreading from the tonsil through the blood may produce abscesses all over the body, or may simply stop with the tonsil; the same germ that produces inflammation of the joints (so-called rheumatism), may pass to the heart, grow there, and growing there cause what used to be called rheumatic heart. The germ of syphilis may kill its host by destroying the liver, or the blood vessels, or the kidney, or the brain. Many cases of "Bright's disease" are caused by syphilis, which likewise may destroy the eyes of the patient if it be growing in the eye. Scores of text books of pathology have been written for the instruction of students and physicians in the details of how all these things—and many more—are accomplished by the germs of disease growing in the body.

When large numbers of persons in a community are highly susceptible to a disease germ, and this disease germ is easily passed around through some agency that is not directly under the control of man by strict quarantine, say an insect such as a fly, or a louse, or a flea, the community is appalled by an epidemic. An epidemic of disease is only some bacterium or animal organism seen at its best from its own point of view—at its worst from our point of view. But epidemics do not do one-thousandth of the damage or death that is done by the germ that takes its toll continuously, day in and day out, without becoming "epidemic" at all. It is these disease germs that are the hardest in reality to fight, because no quarantine is waged against them at all, nor can ever be waged until all men are made intelligent, and the public conscience is raised to the pitch where an injury to any one person in a community is seen to be a danger that threatens all. How can quarantine or law prevent a man from sneezing and coughing in a crowded public place, when his saliva may be, or is, loaded with destructive germs, unknown to himself or others? But such a "quarantine" would be the only one that would safeguard the people from the diseases carried by them, whether knowingly or not, in their own bodies.

EPIDEMICS

One way to wipe out, or at least suspend infectious diseases would be to render the people immune to them, or at any rate render very large numbers of the people immune and thus break up the track along which the germs are carried, because if numerous islands of immunity are thus established the spread of the germs will stop when, in the course of their spread, they chance upon one of the islands ("islands" meaning im-

mune individuals or groups of them). The hope
of being able to do this raised its head high when,
away back in 1890, Behring, the German bacteriologist, discovered the antitoxin for diphtheria.
That was the beginning—the big beginning—of
all the work that has been done in immunity to
infections. This discovery likewise raised the
hope of being able to cure infectious diseases by
means of serums and vaccines, and the whole
world knows what a fuss has been made by this
hope within the past twenty-five years. It also
knows how little has been accomplished by the
activity of the most acute scientists in the world.
Infectious diseases are still with us, and in virtually the same amount as they were previously to
1890, the year when Behring made his discovery.
This does not mean that Behring and the other
bacteriologists of the world were a parcel of fools.
It simply means that all human science has its limitations.

A. T. STILL THE PIONEER IMMUNOLOGIST

Long before Behring, or any other bacteriologist, worked in this line, Dr. Andrew Taylor Still,
the founder of osteopathy, began to treat infections on the principle that the body itself contained the cure, which was virtually the announcement of the theory of immunity; and Still will
ultimately be given credit for this original thought
in the future history of medicine. In former
chapters we have told already how and why
the osteopath secures results in the treatment
of infectious diseases, and have explained how this
treatment is in absolute agreement with the facts

of infection and immunity as science understands these things today. Let us now glance at the results of osteopathic treatment of infectious diseases and the results of laboratory experiments by biological experimentalists from a point of view from which can be seen those peculiar and interesting parallelisms mentioned in the first part of this paper.

First and foremost we make no stupid, ignorant or undemonstrable claim when we say that osteopathic treatment quickly stops the growth of many pathogenic germs in the human body, especially when the infection is treated early in its course. The earlier it is given the treatment the better the results. All osteopaths know this to be true. Now this is precisely what Behring found to be the case with his antitoxin treatment for diphtheria, and it is the one important consideration in the application of the antitoxin in human diphtheria. When the powerful and highly diffusible toxins of the diphtheria organism have destroyed beyond repair vital organs of the body, neither antitoxin nor osteopathy can reconstruct them. Neither antitoxin nor osteopathy can restore the dead to life, and in such hopeless cases the patient is virtually dead long before the heart ceases to beat. But if the treatment (whether antitoxin or osteopathy) be given while there are as yet comparatively little toxins in the blood and the tissues, the antibodies that we must assume are made following osteopathic treatment which lowers tissue tension along the spine, caused by the toxins, and thus releases the nerves—these antibodies, we say, quickly neutralize the toxins, just because there is but a small quantity of them as yet present. In other words, it is easier to repel the small advance of an invading army than it is to save the country after a horde of the enemy have ravaged and sacked it and killed half the population.

The lesson to be learned here is simply this, that osteopathic treatment, in all the infections it is known to stop and cure, acts precisely as the antitoxin cure acts in diphtheria.

But this is only the first of the parallelisms we have in mind, and it is the most striking because the antitoxin for diphtheria is the only serum that has given any degree whatever of satisfaction or assurance of results even under the most favorable human conditions.

DIPHTHERIA

Antitoxin for diphtheria is made by growing diphtheria germs in bouillon for several weeks, killing the germs, allowing the bacteria to settle to the bottom of the flask, and then using the fluid bouillon (which contains the toxins) for injection in increasing doses into horses, until the serum of the horse is found to be sufficiently antitoxic to the toxin. One unit of antitoxin (according to the classic formula) is as much of the antitoxin as will neutralize 100 doses of the toxin, one of which will kill a 250-gram guinea pig in 96 hours.

Now this principle and procedure have been found to work well enough in diphtheria, and then only in the earlier stages of the disease, before the toxin has killed too much body tissue, but they do not work at all in any other infection. Bacteriologists and immunologists have ransacked the whole world to duplicate the results of diphtheria antitoxin in other infectious diseases (even in alcohol and drug habits) but have everywhere and all of the time failed! Small claims of success in small percentages have been made by the men who have originated some such serums, but not one of such serums has stood up! Serums have been made for all infections, but do you hear much about them? The fact that you do not hear about them is evidence enough, you can be assured, that such serums have not stood the practical tests even in slight degree, the diphtheria serum, the great king of them all, being heard of only in a way not altogether and completely satisfactory even as yet—twenty-eight years after its discovery, and full twenty-four years after its general introduction and use in all the lands of Christendom.

The anti-typhoid vaccine (not serum) now being used as a preventive of typhoid, seems to be giving excellent results, especially as used in the world's armies; but (as is the case with smallpox vaccination) its uses are entirely prophylactic (not curative) and it would be of no service if administered after one had actually contracted typhoid fever.

Let us take the germ that causes lobar pneumonia—the pneumococcus of Fraenkel (who discovered it). Some—many—of the best immunologists of Europe and America have tried to make a serum which will neutralize the pneumonia toxin and cause the germs to die out in the tissues, but have failed beyond help. No use. The same attempts have been made with the germ that causes typhoid fever, but today there is no serum for typhoid fever. Serums have been tried for bubonic plague and other infections—virtually for all infections—with much the same issue. The results have all been so shadowy, so uncertain, so very here and there in their character, that any one who has common sense, to say nothing of scientific knowledge, is disposed to shrug the shoulders and fall back into the waiting line. What we want is a serum that will cure in the earliest stages—not a serum that, being given at the natural crisis of the disease "cures" patients that were just about to sit up in bed of their own natural desire and ask for bread and beefsteak! No serums of that kind will ever be talked about for more than long enough to allow the discoverer to state his methods of manufacture and promptly retire, the patient being up and engaged in his daily occupation in the meantime!

But theoretically all these serums should be in use and doing good work right along.

Now is it not strange that just those very diseases which theoretically should fall in the domain of serum cures are the very diseases which have been found to yield to osteopathic treatment when that treatment is administered early in the infection, for no osteopath would claim to have cured pneumonia or typhoid fever, when he had treated that disease just before the natural crisis, when the patient's body cells had succeeded in making

the needed amount of antibodies to neutralize the
toxins and to cause the germs to die out in the
tissues.

Osteopaths are not afraid to collect the vital
statistics in cases of pneumonia and typhoid fever
which have been treated at the beginning of the
invasion. Such statistics are by no means as complete as the osteopathic profession would like
them to be, but there are sufficient privately gathered statistics of that kind to warrant the private
conviction of numerous osteopaths that pneumonia and typhoid fever yield quickly to the treatment when early given, and the riper and fuller
such statistics grow the clearer does the truth become that shines through them—uncertain as all
statistics of this kind must inevitably be in favor
of or against the conclusions that men (whether
advocates or opponents) draw from them.

Our desire was mainly to show that the theory
of immunologists runs parallel with the practical
results which osteopathy finds in its treatment of
infectious diseases. Many diseases which should
be curable by serums (or vaccines) and are not,
are found to be curable by osteopathic treatment,
and osteopaths are ready, and have been ready
many years, to submit to control conditions in
testing the virtue of osteopathy in such diseases in
a public trial, in picked cases, in a public hospital,
on even terms with the best and fairest minded
gentlemen in the medical profession—could such
men be induced for a few days to abandon their
prejudices and submit to a practical trial for the
establishment of fact.

But while osteopaths at all times have been perfectly willing to submit to such a test of the virtue of their art and science, such a test would and could not be entirely satisfactory, any more than a similar test would be satisfactory in deciding upon the virtue of a serum cure. For such a trial, after all, would only be the application of the statistical method, and this method is at best a most insecure one, whether the interpretation of the results be favorable or the reverse. Long periods of time and a careful keeping of records are essential in determining the utility of any cure, or other biological reaction, unless the reaction be almost invariable; in which case the variations from the rule must be promptly understood and accounted for. The ideal method of testing osteopathy, as well as other reactions in these things, is the laboratory experimental method, when all conditions and facts are directly under the control of the experimenter, and the results, when obtained, can absolutely be reproduced at the will of the operator, such as the time when the infection goes in, the uniformity of the individuals tested, the uniformity of the conditions under which these individuals live at the time of the experiment, and have lived previously to the experiment, the material (that is, the infective material) injected, and the uniformity of the subsequent and experimental treatment and results.

The lower animals alone offer such ideal subjects of experiment, and the results in the use of such animals can be depended upon absolutely as a sure clew to the manner in which the treatment, whatever it is, can be assumed to act in the human body also, if it be possible to apply it. For that reason the osteopathic profession does not assert that laboratory experiments on animals are useless or misleading. This, indeed, was the position which the medical profession took strongly, and fought viciously, when biologists some years ago began to teach that drugs were always harmful to man just because they found in their experiments that drugs were always harmful to the lower animals. The medical doctors turned on these scientific pharmacologists (working in the universities, and distinctly not medical men at all) and fiercely denounced them for their teaching.

"You teach that drugs are harmful to man," the medical men said, "because you find them harmful to animals? But guinea pigs, rabbits, dogs and cats are not men, and you have no right to conclude that because drugs are found to injure guinea pigs and dogs, they are therefore injurious to man, and that they should not be given for the cure of diseases in the human body. You have no business drawing such conclusions. Guinea pigs and rabbits are not human beings, and just because drugs injure guinea pigs and dogs, you should not be allowed to teach that they injure man".

But the biologists had demonstrated, and are still demonstrating, a great fact, just the same, by their experiments on animals with drugs. They are still teaching their conclusions as facts and today the doctor who would use the argument quoted (which was loud in the mouths of all ignorant doctors twenty or even fifteen years ago) would be put down as an old-fogy ignorant mossback to whom no well-informed modern physician of any school would pay the slightest attention. The biologists in the universities of the world (who are not medical men at all—only scientific searchers for the facts, having no ax but the ax of truth to grind) have battered down the drug superstition by those very same experiments on animals, and by these experiments on animals have proved that drugs are always poison not only to animals but to man too. By their use of the guinea pig, the rabbit and the dog they have forced the medical profession to line up anew on the drug question, and every popular article in every popular magazine and newspaper (written by medical doctors today) warns the public against the doctor who gives drugs (with perhaps two or three exceptions) to the human body in the hope of curing disease.

No! Those who say that the osteopathic profession argues against the conclusions of science from experiments on lower animals to man are very unjust to the scientific attitude of that profession. And if, here and there, an osteopath is found who makes such an argument, he is probably under the influence of the old medical idea in that line, and is himself doing an injustice to the high scientific conscience of his own profession, as well as to the conscience and power of the world's best and most conservative scientific thinkers and experimentalists, who seek only the facts as they can be found by the best scientific methods known to men today.

Indeed, so far is the great osteopathic profession from holding any such antiquated and ignorant view, that it has put up out of its own hard and honestly earned money a great sum to endow its Research Institute in Chicago for the very purpose, among others, of using animal experiments to forward our knowledge of the results of osteopathic treatment. And this national Research Institute, supported by the money earned in the treatment of human disease by individual osteopathic practitioners, has, during the four years of its existence, used the lower animals continuously in the experiments which the workers in it have made, and are making, to develop osteopathic treatment and to draw conclusions about the effects of osteopathic treatment in man from the results of experiments made upon the lower animals. And this Institute, in time, should grow and develop, and will, it is sincerely hoped and believed, be for osteopathic science what the general movement of research has been for science in general during the past century, and especially during the past twenty-five years, in which time this very kind of research has forced a re-ordering and a deep and great reform in all opinion and belief concerning disease and its treatment in man and the lower animals.

INDEX

Abderhalden, 30.
Abderhalden, test for pregnancy, 68.
Acne, 75
Acquapendente, Fabricio ab, 5.
Adjustment, osteopathic, 180.
Adjuvants, 183.
Age. the, in which Still entered upon his medical researches, 18-23.
Altmann, 34.
American School of Osteopathy, 16, 17.
Angina pectoris, mistaken diagnosis of, 99.
Animal experimentation, 14, 16, 196.
Animal experimentation alone exact and dependable, 208.
Animal experimentation destroyed the dogma of drug therapy, 210.
Animal experimentation, osteopathic research thru, 211.
Animal experimentation results in, 51
Animal experimentation vindicated, 208.
Anodynes, injury from in treating "rheumatism," 95.
Antibodies, 64, 65, 70, 71, 85.
Antibodies, formation of, 149.
Antibodies, osteopathic increase and activation of, 150, 153, 154.
Antibodies, produced by osteopathic stimulation, 56.
"Antibody content" of blood, a normal secretion, 56.
Antitoxins, 197, 180.
Antitoxins, discovery of, 5.
Antitoxins, how made, 204.
Antityphoid vaccine, 188, 189.
Antityphoid vaccine useless after typhoid is contracted, 205.
Appendicitis, 190.
Artery, the rule of, supreme, 29.
Arthritis, gonorrheal, 110.
Arthritis, rheumatoid, 112.

Bacteremia, 73.
Bacteria, 196.
Bacteria, nature of, 121.
Baer, von, 20, 22.
Becquerel, 15.
Behring, von, 5, 30, 202.
Behring, von, found the early administration of anti-toxin in diphtheria imperative, 203.
Bennett, 4, 50.
Bennett, first compelled abandonment of bleeding, 5.
Bernard, Claude, 20, 22.
Bernard's theory, all ingested substances either food or poisons, 20.
Biologists are not medical physicians, 210.
Blood as the agent of metabolism, 140.
Blood, carries the body's healing, 28.

Blood, circulation disturbed through spinal lesions, 11, 12.
Blood, clotting, history of, 141.
Blood, poisoning, 73.
"Blood seed" theory, Still's, anticipated "blastema" theory", 33.
Body resistance, 58, 59.
Boils, 75, 82.
Boils and acne vaccine, 187
Boils, infrequent susceptibility to, 199.
Body chemism, 170.
Body chemism, what interferes with it should not enter the body, 174.
Body contains all its own "medicines," 8.
Body makes its own medicines, 179.
Bordet, 30, 73, 145.
Bordet's blood researches, 158, 159.
Bowman, 22.
Bronchitis, 179.
Bronchitis, chronic, when due to heart, spinal or rib lesions, 182.
Brown-Sequard, 57.
Bubonic plague, 206.
Buchner, 30.
Bucher, blood researcher, 146.
Bursitis, 99.

Cancer, serum test for, 68.
Catarrh, 180.
Cells, all other, are slaves of the nerve cells, 176.
Cells, as intermediaries between nerve fibrils and blood elements, 141.
"Cell theory" of Schwann, 19.
Cerebro-spinal meningitis, 181.
Chemisms, body, 55.
Chemism of body is nerve controlled, 137.
Cholera bacilli, killed by normal blood serum, 145, 146.
"Cold", common, so-called, presents same sort of phenomena of immunity in recovery as typhoid, 157.
"Cold", simple, 179
Colitis, 190.
Colon bacillus, 74, 200, 202.
Commercial drug houses' exaggerated claims, 184.
Contageous disease, what the term means, 197.
Contractures of spinal tissue, 43.
"Controls", or "control experiments" in typhoid research, 153.
Counter irritants 35.
Cure, only rational, lies in the nature of the tissues and blood themselves, 157, 158, 160.
Cures, research investigators make no claims of, 155.
Cures, so-called, by animal serums and vaccines, usually applied by doctors ignorant of their nature, 155, 156.

212

INDEX

213

INDEX

INDEX

Osteopathy not massage, 55.
Osteopathy offers alluring field for laboratory experiment, 56.
Osteopathy promotes immunity, 89, 90.
Osteopathy routs infectious diseases by increasing blood flow, 166.
Osteopathy stops the growth of many pathogenic germs, 203.
Osteopathy tested clinically, 10.
Osteopathy upheld by all biologic discovery, 165.
Osteopathy, why it is a drugless system, 166.
Osteopathy works like antitoxin in diphtheria, 203, 204.

Pains, osteopathy available for when of mechanical or germ origin, 113.
Pasteur, 9, 19, 22.
Pathology, experimental, works along osteopathic lines, 186.
Pathology, modern, birth of, 7.
Pfeiffer, 30, 145.
Pfeiffer's phenomenon of rising immunity in the animal body against living cholera germs, 146, 147.
Pharmacological maxim, chemically active substances ingested are either foods or poisons, 49, 175.
Pharmacological research arose long after Still's new therapy, 51.
Pharmacology at length exploded drug therapy, 52.
Pharmacology's discredit of drugging met with the violent opposition of physicians, 51-52.
Pharmacologists were denounced by physicians, 209, 210.
Phagocytes, 163, 179, 180.
Plague, 180.
Pneumonia, 27, 179.
Pneumococcus, 200.
Pneumococcus of Fraenkel, 205.
Poison, 175.
Poisons, all active ingested substances not foods are, 49, 175.
Predisposing cause of disease, 59.
Principle, the, underlying vaccine and osteopathic therapy are identical, 68.
Prostatitis, 191.
Protein, 173.
Protoplasm, 173.
Protozoa, 196.
Protozoan diseases, smallpox and syphilis, 196.
Pus, 80.
Pus, how formed, 165.
Pus pockets in tissues, 107, 108.

Ramsay, 15.
Raymond, 22.
Research, all, supports Still's main theories, 10.
Research, European, confirms Still's teachings, 26, 58.
Research Institute, The A. T. Still, 16, 211.
Research investigators do not seek especially to find "cures," 162, 164.

Research, modern blood, vindicates the supreme intuitions of Still, 185.
Research, osteopathic, 56.
Research, osteopathic, into influenza, 61, 64.
"Colds", 62.
Research workers, European, vindicate theory and practice of Still, 26, 58.
Resistance increases the moment disease begins, 59.
Resistance, natural, increased by osteopathy, 64.
Resistance, natural, released by tissue adjustment or stimulation, 60.
Resistance, osteopathic increase of, 91.
"Rheumatism", 94, 189, 190.
"Rheumatism," articular, early osteopathic administration in, 106.
Rheumatism, articular or infectious varieties of, 102.
"Rheumatism", caused by lesions, 98.
Rheumatism, infectious, no serum or vaccine effective in, 105.
"Rheumatism", so-called, really many different ills, 96.
"Rheumatism", varieties of, osteopathy is available for, 107.
Rib, twisted, cause of breast and arm pain, 99.
Rule, the, of the artery supreme, 29.

Scarlet fever, 27, 74, 179.
Schick test for diphtheria anti-bodies, 68.
Schwann, Theodor, 19, 22, 33, 34.
Schwann, Theodor, as a forerunner of osteopathy, 122, 137.
Schwann, Theodor, discoverer of cellular anatomy, 116, 154.
Schwann, Theodor, discoverer of pepsin, 20.
Sciatica, caused by twisted pelvis, 101.
Scientific men themselves are not drug takers, 183.
Septicemia, highly virulent streptococcic, 73.
Septicemia, 74, 103.
Septicemia, rapid action of toxins, 74.
Serum investigators have made no great claims, 184.
Serum therapy's claims summarized, 187.
Serum test for cancer, 68.
Serum therapy, its beginning, 183.
Serum therapy regarded as a "worked out" mine, 188.
Serums and vaccines are not true drugs, 49.
Serums and vaccines, 90 per cent of claims for, false, 72.
Serums and vaccines overplayed by ignorant doctors, 72.
Serums and vaccines practically fail to cure infections, 67.
Serum and vaccine therapy possibilities regarded as now exhausted, 188.
Sleep neutralizes fatigue toxins, 93.
Smallpox, 27, 74, 180.

215

INDEX

216

INDEX